Casebook Plus

for

Fagin

Criminal Justice

prepared by

Clarence Augustus Martin
California State University, Dominguez Hills

Tere L. Chipman
Fayetteville Technical Community College

Boston   New York   San Francisco
Mexico City   Montreal   Toronto   London   Madrid   Munich   Paris
Hong Kong   Singapore   Tokyo   Cape Town   Sydney

ISBN 0-205-37924-9

Printed in the United States of America

10 9 8 7 6 5 4 3   08 07 06 05 04 03

TABLE OF CONTENTS

POWERPOINT LECTURE NOTES:

CHAPTER 1: THE CRIMINAL JUSTICE DISCIPLINE

CASE

The reality of what it means to pursue a career in criminal justice is sometimes not clearly understood by laypersons. People who are not in the profession form personal opinions about and images of what it means to be a law enforcement professional. Some of these opinions and images are unrealistic in their expectations. Those who receive degrees in higher education are better prepared to enter into law enforcement because they understand the fundamental theoretical, administrative, and historical issues that inform the American approach to law enforcement.

Because of the humanistic quality of the administration of justice and because of the many careers that comprise the criminal justice system, students can feel weighed down by theoretical explanations of real-life situations. This is understandable, considering the many different types of law enforcement agencies, the many levels of law enforcement, and the fact that the United States has many hundreds of law enforcement agencies with their own idiosyncratic qualities.

It is therefore important for students to take full advantage of criminal justice internships. Internships are good "reality checks" that will assist students in developing a mature and accurate understanding of what it means to be a law enforcement professional. This is the kind of experience that, if properly developed, can be a capstone for one's undergraduate education. A well-implemented internship program will apply classroom theories to actual practice in the field and demonstrate what is expected of participants in a professional environment. Experiences might include patrol station ride-alongs, custody issues, crime labs, traffic accident roll-outs, detective services, arson/explosives, and other important issues. When participating in this kind of educational experience, the best way for students to develop an overall understanding of the value of their internships is to keep an intern journal. Journals allow participants to thread their day-to-day experiences into a comprehensive whole.

Definitions:

Criminal justice internship: A practicum that assigns students to law enforcement agencies for a professional and "real-life" exposure to the law enforcement profession.

Intern journal: A daily log that is useful for evaluating the internship experience.
Patrol station ride-alongs: The assignment of students to police cruisers as observers to experience the typical daily routine of patrol officers.

Traffic accident roll-outs: The assignment of students to emergency response teams that specialize in traffic emergencies.

CRITICAL THINKING: YOU DECIDE

Assume that you have been assigned to a patrol station ride-along. On one of your days with the patrol officers, you are called to the scene of a domestic dispute. As they try to de-escalate the situation (which is occurring outside of the home), you notice that young children inside the home are crying and watching the confrontation. One of them beckons you over to a window. What should you do? Should you try to calm down the child? Should you participate in this incident in any way?

_____

_____

_____

_____

_____

What are reasonable parameters for participation?

_____

_____

_____

_____

_____

_____

ESSAY: ETHICS AND DISCRETION

Assume that you are participating in a patrol ride-along. Assume further that during the ride-along, the officers make an arrest but begin to engage in unprofessional behavior. They verbally abuse the suspect and drag her around by her hair. What should you do?

_____

_____

_____

_____

_____

Should you talk to the officers about their behavior? Should you talk to their superiors? What would you say?

_____

_____

_____

_____

_____

CASE OUTCOME

Criminal justice internships are invaluable educational experiences. In a practical sense, students can identify what kind of law enforcement assignment interests them the most. At the same time, law enforcement agencies can entice well-educated candidates into their applicant pools.

ONLINE INVESTIGATION: THE INSIDE STORY

For an online search of criminal justice professions, students should enter general keywords, such as "criminalist" and "forensic psychologist."

FYI: CAREER CONNECTION

For information about internship opportunities, contact local law enforcement agencies and local university advisement offices.

CHAPTER 2: THE CRIMINAL JUSTICE PROCESS

CASE

The juvenile justice process is a multidisciplinary subject that requires a general understanding of interlinkages between the broader community, the American justice system, and the juvenile justice system. Several disciplines impact the juvenile justice process, including sociology, psychology, and the law. The juvenile justice system is the system through which minors are processed. It encompasses a broad community of agencies and programs. The system is an administrative network for processing youths who violate the law or who are abused, abandoned or neglected; in theory, the system seeks to protect juveniles, not punish them.

The juvenile justice system has historically processed cases of juvenile delinquency and status offenses. Society is now confronted by a relatively new debate–that of trying minors as adults. More violent offenders and those participating in organized criminal enterprises, such as street gangs, are being processed through the criminal justice system. The trend in most states is to incorporate some type of waiver and certification into their juvenile justice and criminal procedures, whereby juvenile and criminal courts have concurrent jurisdiction over some offenses. Waiver is when the juvenile court waives jurisdiction and transfers the case to criminal court. Certification occurs when the juvenile is certified as an adult by the juvenile court or prosecutor for the purposes of criminal prosecution. The effects of waiver and certification are that juveniles are tried as adults, are subject to the same court proceedings and constitutional protections as adults, and receive adult penalties.

Certifying juveniles as adults for prosecution in the criminal justice system can be a controversial solution to the problem of juvenile criminal behavior. One criticism is that it takes young people out of the safety net set up to rehabilitate juvenile offenders, and places them into a system where the emphasis is on punishment. Another criticism is that this philosophy is causing a criminalization of juvenile court, thus allowing juvenile courts to practice punishment, rather than rehabilitation.

Definitions:

Juvenile justice agency: "A government agency…of which the functions are the investigation, supervision, adjudication, care, or confinement of juvenile offenders and nonoffenders subject to the jurisdiction of a juvenile court."[1]

Juvenile certification: The process whereby a juvenile is certified as an adult by the juvenile court or prosecutor for the purposes of criminal prosecution.

---

[1] Rush, George E. *The Dictionary of Criminal Justice*, 5th ed. New York: Dushkin/McGraw Hill, 2000. Page 189.

Juvenile waiver: The process whereby the juvenile court waives jurisdiction and transfers the case to criminal court.

CRITICAL THINKING: YOU DECIDE

Assume that you are a social worker for a juvenile justice agency. One of your cases involves a young offender who has been repeatedly in trouble with the authorities for assault, drug trafficking, and truancy. He has always been processed through the system as a juvenile delinquent. You know that his home situation is very dysfunctional, with parental substance abuse and emotional detachment. Would you recommend that he continue to be brought into the juvenile justice system rather than certify him as an adult in the criminal justice system? Why?

_____

_____

_____

_____

_____

_____

What would your recommendation be if his anti-social behavior has just begun to be expressed by anger and violence?

_____

_____

_____

_____

ESSAY: ETHICS AND DISCRETION

Assume that you are a juvenile justice officer investigating a case on behalf of the juvenile court. The juvenile court is weighing whether to waive jurisdiction over the juvenile in question, thus sending her into the jurisdiction of the adult criminal court. The juvenile repeatedly stabbed a male teacher in her high school, yelling "I am going to kill you!" The teacher is in critical condition and may not survive his injuries. You discover that the girl has been sexually assaulted and beaten repeatedly by her father, and that the adults in her family have done nothing to stop the abuse. You also discover that she has run away from home on two occasions, but that the police have used their discretion to return her home. What factors would you weigh prior to making your recommendation to the court? What alternatives might you consider for this girl?

_____

_____

_____

_____

_____

_____

_____

CASE OUTCOME

The juvenile justice system is much more interventionist than the adult criminal justice system. It is more flexible and offers a broad range of services to intervene in the lives of troubled juveniles. Its underlying philosophy is one of rehabilitation. However, with the rise in violent juvenile behavior, and because of the shift in the nation's philosophy against adult offenders, most states now regularly try juveniles as adults for certain offenses. In some states, juveniles will be automatically certified as adults, depending on the crime and the perpetrator's age.

ONLINE INVESTIGATION: THE INSIDE STORY

For an online search of issues confronting the juvenile justice system, students should enter the keywords, "juvenile justice" and "juvenile delinquency" to bring up Web sites and reports that discuss juvenile justice issues.

FYI: CAREER CONNECTION

For information about careers in juvenile justice, including social work, access the Web pages of both governmental and private juvenile justice agencies in your state and locality.

Students should also access the Web site of Office of Juvenile Justice and Delinquency Prevention at http://ojjdp.ncjrs.org/.

CHAPTER 3: CRIMINAL BEHAVIOR: DEFINITIONS AND CAUSES

CASE

Crime on campus was at one time an undiscussed area of criminal justice. It was something that was rarely reported unless a significant incident occurred on campus, and most incidents were handled "in house" by university administrators and campus police. Student newspapers did not print crime statistics because university administrators and police would not give them the data. This has changed, with colleges now waging vigorous awareness campaigns on campus and student newspapers have access to crime statistics.

Hate crimes are broadly defined as crimes that are motivated by hatred against particular classes of people. Thus, if an aggravated assault has racial bias as its motive, it is a hate crime. Hate crimes on campus are particularly volatile issues. Because of the theoretical position of universities as bastions of reasoned discourse, hate crimes seemingly attack more than simply a class of people–these attack the very notion that universities are the "marketplace of ideas." Hundreds of on-campus hate crimes are reported each year. These crimes occur in different ways: Some involve hate posters or signs, others are of the aggressive "name-calling" variety, and others are violent. Administrators and campus police have investigated hate crimes regularly with great vigor.

One troubling quality of these crimes on campus is that some of these are criminal hoaxes. Hate crime hoaxes have occurred on a number of campuses, including Duke University, the University of Georgia, Guilford College, Eastern New Mexico University, St. Cloud State, and Miami University of Ohio. In the latter case, about fifty racist flyers were taped neatly to the walls and computer monitors in a building where African American students socialize. The campus, which already had a reputation for racial polarization, became quite tense. An investigation by the police and fingerprinting analysis by the Ohio Bureau of Criminal Identification and Investigation confirmed that two African American students had perpetrated a hoax.

Definitions:

Campus crime: Criminal incidents that occur on the campuses of public and private institutions of higher learning.

Criminal hoax: The fabrication of a criminal incident with the purpose to have the fabrication falsely reported to law enforcement officials as an actual criminal incident.

Hate crime: Criminal behavior in which "the defendant intentionally selects a victim, or in the case of a property crime, the property that is the object of the crime, because of the actual or perceived race, color, religion, national origin, ethnicity, gender, disability, or sexual orientation of any person."[1]

CRITICAL THINKING: YOU DECIDE

Assume that you are a police officer for a large university. An incident occurs on your campus in which a cross is illegally burned late at night in front of the student union building. This is the signature symbol of the Ku Klux Klan. There have been rumors that a racial supremacist group has been organized within the student body. How would you investigate this incident? Who would you question?

_____

_____

_____

_____

_____

What kind of cooperation would you seek from outside law enforcement agencies? Which agencies would you contact?

_____

_____

_____

_____

_____

_____

---

[1] Rush, George E. *The Dictionary of Criminal Justice*, 5th ed. New York: Dushkin/McGraw-Hill, 2000. Page 159.

ESSAY: ETHICS AND DISCRETION

Assume that you are the lead investigator for sorting through the evidence of the foregoing incident. If your investigation uncovers evidence suggesting that the incident was a hoax perpetrated by fraternity, how would this affect your approach to the incident?

_____

_____

_____

_____

_____

If your investigation uncovers evidence suggesting that the incident was a hoax perpetrated by an on-campus activist organization, how would this affect your approach to the incident?

_____

_____

_____

_____

_____

_____

_____

CASE OUTCOME

The investigation of campus crime in general, and campus hate crimes in particular, require the consideration of factors that are unique to the university setting. Universities are a special kind of community that must balance the interests of administrators, faculty, and students. These factors must be taken into account when on-campus police use standard investigation methods and procedures.

ONLINE INVESTIGATION: THE INSIDE STORY

For an online search of law enforcement issues on college campuses, students should enter the keywords, "campus crime" and "campus police," to bring up Web sites and reports that discuss on-campus crime.

FYI: CAREER CONNECTION

For information about becoming a campus police officer, contact the police office on your campus.

For general data and other information about campus policing and crime, access the U.S. Department of Education, Office of Post-Secondary Education's Web site at http://www.ope.ed.gov/security/.

CHAPTER 4: CRIMINAL LAW: CONTROL VERSUS LIBERTY

CASE

The criminalization of drugs is a behavioral prescription. Drug laws prohibit the possession, usage, and trafficking of certain controlled substances. Although these offenses are technically mala prohibita offenses, drug offenders often receive prison sentences that are as harsh as mala in se offenses.

The "drug war" was declared by the administration of President Ronald Reagan in the early 1980s. Since then, cocaine trafficking has been a major target of the war. It is an international endeavor. For example, the coca plant is mostly grown in Peru and Colombia; processed into powder cocaine in Colombia, transported to the United States by Colombian and Mexican gangs, sold "wholesale" by American drug lords, and distributed "retail" by street gangs and other traffickers.

Cocaine is sold in powder form and "rock" form–the latter is popularly referred to as "crack" cocaine because of the crackling sound it makes when smoked. Powder cocaine is an expensive drug that is usually ingested by sniffing. Crack cocaine is cheap and ingested by smoking. Powder cocaine has been a drug for the well-to-do. When crack cocaine was introduced in the 1980s, it was a tremendous retail success because now anyone could purchase cocaine. Authorities cited it as a reason for a marked increase in drug-related violent crime. In 1986, Congress quickly passed laws that required mandatory minimum five-year sentences for possessing certain amounts of drugs. For powder cocaine, that amount is 500 grams (one-half of a kilo), worth approximately $55,000. For crack cocaine, that amount is five grams (one two-hundredths of a kilo), worth approximately $425.

The incarceration rate for drug offences has increased significantly. By 1998, 58% of all persons serving time in federal prison had been convicted of drug offenses. The mean prison sentence in 1996 for federal drug offenses was sixty-five months.

Definitions:

Mala in se: "[T]hose acts that are immoral or wrong in themselves."[1]

Mala prohibita: "[C]rimes that are made illegal by legislation, as opposed to acts that are crimes because they are considered evil in and of themselves."[2]

---

[1] Rush, George E. *The Dictionary of Criminal Justice*, 5th ed. New York: Dushkin/McGraw-Hill, 2000. Page 204.
[2] Id., page 205.

Mandatory minimum sentence: "A statutory requirement that a certain penalty shall be set and carried out in all cases upon conviction for a specified offense or series of offenses."[3]

CRITICAL THINKING: YOU DECIDE

Assume that you are a special agent of the Drug Enforcement Administration. You have received a tip that a major drug dealer is selling drugs from his home. You and other special agents obtain a warrant and raid the home. You find twenty-five grams of crack cocaine, worth about $2,125 on the street. Is this a "major drug bust?" Why? Is this a good use of your team's resources? Why?

_____

_____

_____

_____

_____

_____

_____

Assume that you are the same DEA special agent. The day after your crack raid, you receive a second tip that another major drug dealer is selling drugs from his home. You and other special agents obtain a warrant and raid the home. You find 500 grams of powder cocaine, worth about $55,000 on the street. In comparison to your previous day's raid, is this a "major drug bust?" Why? Is this a good use of your team's resources? Why?

_____

_____

_____

_____

_____

[3] Id., page 205-206.

What reasons can you think of to maintain the current drug laws on the books? What reasons can you think of to amend current drug laws?

_____

_____

_____

_____

_____

_____

ESSAY: ETHICS AND DISCRETION

The drug war is an accepted national policy. It has required the allocation of massive law enforcement resources to end the drug trade. Assume that you are a member of Congress. You have carefully reviewed the allocation of resources to fight the drug war. Should these resources be maintained? Should more resources be allocated? Should the cocaine sentencing guidelines be restructured? Should these be strengthened? Can we win the drug war? Should it remain a centerpiece of law enforcement policy?

_____

_____

_____

_____

_____

_____

CASE OUTCOME

It quickly became clear to researchers that because crack cocaine is a cheap drug, it is prevalent in poor urban neighborhoods. Most of the persons in those neighborhoods are African Americans and Latinos. Consequently, most people convicted of crack cocaine offenses are members of racial and ethnic minority groups. The amount of crack needed for a mandatory-minimum five-year sentence is little more than the amount needed for a single crack binge. In 1995, a report by the U.S. Sentencing Commission found that African Americans comprised 88% of suspects charged with federal crack offenses.

ONLINE INVESTIGATION: THE INSIDE STORY

For an online search of law enforcement and drugs, students should enter the keywords, "drug war" and "drug policy" to bring up Web sites and reports that discuss the American approach to suppressing the drug trade.

FYI: CAREER CONNECTION

This case involved law enforcement officials and policy makers.

For further information about the federal law enforcement agencies, access the Drug Enforcement Administration's website at http://www.usdoj.gov/dea/.

For further information about national drug policy, access the Office of National Drug Control Policy website at:
http://www.whitehousedrugpolicy.gov/

CHAPTER 5: DUE PROCESS AND POLICE PROCEDURE

CASE

Urban law enforcement officials routinely assign police detectives to investigate crimes and search for criminal suspects. When necessary, big-city police departments form task forces or special units to work particularly alarming cases. These cases receive top priority, and members of the task forces or special units are encouraged to aggressively pursue their leads to find the perpetrator.

In New York City, a special unit of the New York Police Department had been assigned to investigate the whereabouts of a serial rapist. Their investigation led them to a neighborhood in the Bronx. On February 5, 1999, four members of the unit shot and killed Amadou Diallo, an unarmed Guinean-born street vendor, while he stood in the vestibule of his apartment building. It was a case of mistaken identity; he was not the serial rapist. The officers later testified at trial that they thought he was the rapist they had been looking for, and they thought he had reached for a gun. The officers fired forty-one bullets, hitting Amadou Diallo nineteen times. Two officers each fired his weapon sixteen times, one officer fired five times, and one officer fired four times.

Many New Yorkers were outraged by the facts of the incident. It appeared to many residents to be a case of racial abuse, because four white officers had shot at an unarmed black man 41 times and hit him 19 times.

After an investigation into the circumstances of the shooting, the four officers were prosecuted on criminal charges. They were charged with several counts of criminal homicide, and during the trial, the jury considered whether they had possibly committed second-degree murder, manslaughter, or criminally negligent homicide. During deliberations, the jury repeatedly asked the judge for instructions on the elements of first-degree manslaughter. The racially-charged case was moved to upstate New York because of pre-trial publicity.

Definitions:

Deadly Force: The use of life-threatening force. Its use by police is "unconstitutional insofar as…the use of deadly force against fleeing suspects who are unarmed and pose no threat to the officer or third parties."[1]

Discretion: "An authority conferred by law on an official or an agency to act in certain conditions or situations in accordance with the named official's or agency's considered judgment and conscience."[2] Discretion exists at different levels of the criminal justice system, such as police discretion and judicial discretion.

---

[1] Rush, George E. *The Dictionary of Criminal Justice*, 5th ed. New York: Dushkin/McGraw-Hill, 2000. Page 98.
[2] Id, page 109.

Police Discretion: The police "must often decide whether or not or how to—Enforce specific laws…[i]nvestigate specific crimes…[s]earch people, vicinities, buildings…[a]rrest or detain people."[3] The police make these decisions as needed under the circumstances.

Reasonable Suspicion: Suspicion "implies a belief or opinion based upon facts or circumstances which do not amount to proof."[4] The police may stop and question people based on reasonable suspicion.

CRITICAL THINKING: YOU DECIDE

The jury deliberated for three days. Assume that you are a member of the jury. What factors would you use to weigh the reasonableness of the behavior of the officers?

_____

_____

_____

_____

_____

_____

_____

---

[3] Id.
[4] Black, Henry Campbell. *Black's Law Dictionary: Definitions of the Terms and Phrases of American and English Jurisprudence, Ancient and Modern.* Revised 4th ed. St. Paul: West Publishing Co., 1968. At 1616.

Was this indeed a case of racial abuse that rises to the level of criminal culpability? Or, was this simply a matter of good aggressive police work under difficult circumstances? How should they decide these considerations?

_____

_____

_____

_____

_____

What other considerations should be discussed during the jury's deliberations?

_____

_____

_____

_____

_____

_____

ESSAY: ETHICS AND DISCRETION

Assume that the four police officers had reasonably believed that the suspect was in the neighborhood, possibly using an intelligence source that they had successfully used previously. Assume further that they reasonably believed that the suspect lived at or near Amadou Diallo's apartment building.

Was the use of deadly force by the officers a reasonable application of police discretion? Discuss what factors should be considered prior to using deadly force. Also, discuss which options should be exhausted prior to the decision to shoot a suspect under circumstances similar to those presented in this case.

_____

_____

_____

_____

_____

Was the discharge of forty-one rounds a reasonable and proportional use of force under the circumstances? If so, why was it reasonable and proportional? If not, why not, and what would have been a reasonable and proportional use of force?

_____

_____

_____

_____

_____

_____

CASE OUTCOME

After three days of deliberations by the jury, the four police officers were acquitted of all criminal charges. The jury consisted of four Black women, one White woman, and seven White men. A key consideration was whether the prosecutor had shown that the officers possessed the requisite mens rea (criminal state of mind) for the criminal charges. The jury did not think that the prosecution met their burden of proof, and therefore voted unanimously to completely exonerate the defendants of criminal guilt.

ONLINE INVESTIGATION: THE INSIDE STORY

For a general online search, students should enter the keywords, "Amadou Diallo," to bring up Web sites and reports that discuss the case.

Students should also conduct online or library research on media reports from several New York City newspapers. Students should compare articles from these papers. For example, compare reports from *The New York Times* (a national newspaper), the *New York Daily News* and *New York Post* (local tabloid newspapers), and the *Amsterdam News* (a Harlem-based newspaper serving the African-American community). How did these newspapers report the story? How were they different? How were they alike?

FYI: CAREER CONNECTION

This case involved professionals from within the criminal justice system that exist in every large metropolitan area. In this case, these professionals included the New York Police Department and the Bronx County District Attorney's Office.

For further information about the NYPD, visit their Web site at http://www.ci.nyc.ny.us/html/nypd/home.html.

For further information about the Bronx County District Attorney, visit their Web site at http://www.bronxda.net/.

CASE

"Organized crime" is a continuing association of people who engage in an illegal enterprise for profit. The most famous organized crime groups include La Cosa Nostra in the United States, the Sicilian Mafia, Japanese Yakuza gangs, Chinese Triad groups, Latin American drug cartels, and the Russian Mafia. Other types of criminal enterprises in the United States include Jamaican posses, urban drug gangs, and the Dixie Mafia. Because of the sophistication of many of these enterprises and the enormous profits that they generate, law enforcement agencies in the United States have never been able to permanently eliminate them. Although many criminal enterprises have been shut down and many individuals have been incarcerated, the allure of high-stakes illicit profits has kept these groups very much in business.

One weapon in the law enforcement arsenal against organized crime is asset forfeiture. It is a procedure whereby law enforcement agencies seize the profits derived from illegal activities. Asset forfeiture laws exist at the state and federal levels and are an outgrowth of legislation that targeted organized criminal influence on private industry. The best known of these acts is the Racketeer Influenced and Corrupt Organizations Act (RICO). Since the passage of RICO, asset forfeiture has been used extensively in the drug war to seize the assets of criminal enterprises.

Law enforcement agencies use two types of asset forfeiture–criminal forfeiture and civil forfeiture. Criminal forfeiture requires prosecutors to prove beyond a reasonable doubt that seized property "relates back" to a *specific* criminal (usually drug) transaction. Civil forfeiture only requires prosecutors to prove by preponderance of the evidence that property relates back to *any* drug-related or other criminal transaction.

Because of the power that asset forfeiture laws give to law enforcement agencies, it has been at the center of controversy about civil liberties issues and the power of the state.

Definitions:

Asset forfeiture: "The governmental seizure of personal assets obtained from or used in a criminal enterprise."[1]

Civil forfeiture: The governmental seizure of personal assets obtained from or used in a criminal enterprise via a civil proceeding.

Criminal forfeiture: The governmental seizure of personal assets obtained from or used in a criminal enterprise via a criminal proceeding.

---

[1] Champion, Dean J. *The American Dictionary of Criminal Justice: Key Terms and Major Court Cases*. Los Angeles: Roxbury Publishing Company, 2001. Page 11.

Organized crime: "Those self-perpetuating, structured associations of individuals and groups combined for the purpose of profiting in whole or in part by illegal means, while protecting their activities through a pattern of graft and corruption."[2]

RICO Act: "Passed by Congress in 1970 to attack organized crime and prosecute it. Also authorizes both civil and criminal asset forfeiture.[3]

CRITICAL THINKING: YOU DECIDE

Assume that you are on the city council of a medium-sized city in Florida, and for the past 5 years the police department of your city has made numerous drug arrests. Assume further that as a result of these arrests the local police department has seized various properties and cash related to these drug violations under the provisions of the asset forfeiture law. The provisions of the asset forfeiture law provide that the arresting police agency can receive 25% to 50% of the value of the property seized. Assume that the police department has received approximately $1 million dollars per year in asset forfeiture revenues for the last 5 years. At the budget hearings a resolution is introduced to cut the proposed police budget by $1.25 million under the assumption that the police could make up this cut by supplementing their budget by asset forfeiture revenues. Would you support this resolution? Why? If police funding is based upon the amount of revenue that they receive from asset forfeiture, does this promote aggressive drug busts that may violate citizen's constitutional rights.

_____

_____

_____

_____

_____

_____

[2] Id., page 97.
[3] Id., page 113.

If the budget of the police department is cut do you think that the police may be tempted to use the potential for asset forfeiture revenue as one of major criteria for enforcing drug laws? What if the police budget were cut by $2 million and the police chief were told to double the amount of revenue he or she obtained through asset forfeiture to make up the difference? Is this an abuse of the asset forfeiture law? Why?

_____

_____

_____

_____

_____

ESSAY: ETHICS AND DISCRETION

Asset forfeiture is an effective strategy in fighting against organized crime because it eliminates the proceeds of illicit enterprises. Assume that you are a U.S. Treasury agent and have the task of tracing the proceeds of a high-ranking La Cosa Nostra *capo*, or captain. He has invested his profits in real estate, including a modest house that he bought for his elderly parents on prime real estate in Florida. He has furnished it for them, and given them an automobile. Assume that they have made the house their only place of residence for a number of years, and have nothing to do with the *capo*'s La Cosa Nostra activities. Should you seize their house? Should you seize their furniture and the automobile? What if they have nowhere to go and very few assets? What if they are also in poor health? Should you advocate the seizure of *all* proceeds of the *capo*'s criminal activities? Should you be selective? Why?

_____

_____

_____

_____

CASE OUTCOME

Although asset forfeiture is an effective law enforcement weapon against organized crime – because it "hits them where it hurts" – it is controversial. Because of this, several Supreme Court decisions have delimited the parameters of asset forfeiture. For example, in *U.S. v. Usury*, 116 S.Ct. 2135, 135 L.Ed. 2d 549 (1996), the court held that civil forfeiture is *not* a type of *double jeopardy*. Another case is *U.S. v. 92 Buena Vista Avenue*, 113 S.Ct. 1126, L.Ed. 2d 469 (1993), wherein the Court accepted an "innocent owner" defense, which prohibited the government from seizing crime-related property that was later obtained by an innocent owner.

ONLINE INVESTIGATION: THE INSIDE STORY

For an online search of organized crime and asset forfeiture, students should enter the keywords, "organized crime" and "asset forfeiture," to bring up websites and reports that discuss the problem of organized crime and the pro's and con's of asset forfeiture.

FYI: CAREER CONNECTION

This case involved law enforcement investigators.

For further information about U.S. Department of the Treasury's law enforcement bureaus, including Alcohol, Tobacco and Firearms and the U.S. Secret Service, access their Web site at http://www.ustreas.gov/bureaus.html.

CHAPTER 7: ROLES AND FUNCTIONS OF THE POLICE

CASE

The police are charged with protecting the public's safety against those who prey upon society. Their duty is to uphold the law by de-escalating uncontrolled confrontations, resolve criminal incidents, take wrongdoers into custody, and investigate unsolved crimes. These duties require police officers to respond to an innumerable variety of situations, many of them unique circumstances that they have not experienced before. Thus, in the performance of their duties the police must make many on-the-scene decisions about which course of action to follow. Discretionary decisions for police officers include weighing whether or not to search people, whether to enter a building or a residence, whether to investigate specific crimes, how to investigate specific crimes, and whether or not to arrest or detain people. This discretionary authority is conferred by law.

Sometimes instinct is a life-saving exercise of discretion. In Cleveland in 1963, a police detective approached several men who were lurking "suspiciously" near a liquor store. His discretionary instinct suggested that the men were about to engage in criminal activity. The officer identified himself, patted them down, conducted a more thorough search, and found weapons – .38 caliber revolvers – on two of the suspects. The men were arrested on charges of illegally carrying concealed weapons. This incident led to an important Supreme Court decision, *Terry v. Ohio*, which established standards for what has come to be called a Terry stop or Terry pat-down.

A number of factors affect the police in their calculation about how to proceed in a particular situation. Official standards for discretionary authority such as department policies or training will naturally guide the exercise of discretion. Unofficial standards such as personal considerations can also impact discretionary authority. For example, the attributes of a suspect such as race or gender could affect discretion. Or, politically sensitive issues in a community such as prostitution or drug trafficking could cause an officer to either detain or ignore a suspect. Or, unofficial cultures of a police department or station house such as unofficial crackdowns on gangs could also affect discretionary decisions.

Definitions:

Police discretion: Authority conferred on the police to exercise his or her judgment in performing law enforcement duties, such as conducting searches or detaining suspects.

CRITICAL THINKING: YOU DECIDE

Training and professionalism are critical elements in the proper exercise of police discretion. Higher education also improves critical thinking skills that an officer can apply to real-life situations. Should different discretionary standards be expected of officers, depending on the quality of training they have received?

_____

_____

_____

_____

_____

Should officers with less training, or lower-quality training be held to a different level of responsibility for discretionary decisions? If so, what standard of responsibility should be applied?

_____

_____

_____

_____

_____

ESSAY: ETHICS AND DISCRETION

Assume that you are a police officer in a demographically homogeneous county in a rural area. You are called as backup to a traffic stop. When you arrive, you find several officers standing over several suspects who are spread-eagled on the ground. All of the suspects are of a different demographic group than the predominant one found in the county. After a thorough search of the individuals and their vehicle, your fellow officers let them go. They later said that it was a "routine" stop of "those kind of people" who drive through the county. What discretionary issues arise in this scenario?

_____

_____

_____

_____

_____

CASE OUTCOME

In *Terry v. Ohio*, 393 U.S. 1 (1968), the Supreme Court ruled that reasonable suspicion is a justifiable standard to conduct a pat-down search. The Supreme Court decision gave six rules for exercising this discretion: First, reasonable suspicion must exist; second, the suspicion is that the suspect could be armed and dangerous; third, the police must identify themselves; fourth, the police may question the suspect; fifth, the officers' fear for safety is not dispelled by the suspect's answers; and sixth, the police conduct a pat-down of the outer clothing.

ONLINE INVESTIGATION: THE INSIDE STORY

For an online search of police discretion, students should enter the keywords, "police discretion" and "search and seizure."

FYI: CAREER CONNECTION

For further information about police forces and their guidelines, access the state police Web site and the state's attorney general Web site for your state of residence.

Students should also access the Web site of the National Association of Attorneys General at http://www.naag.org/.

Or, access the Web site of the International Association of Chiefs of Police at http://www.theiacp.org/.

CHAPTER 8: POLICE PROFESSIONALISM AND THE COMMUNITY

CASE

Community policing embraces the philosophy of the police as service providers. It is a concept that attempts to reduce police isolation from the community and to improve the image of the police at the community level. Several acronyms represent the application of this philosophy: POP for Problem-Oriented Policing, COP for Community-Oriented Policing, and CAPS for Chicago's Alternative Policing Strategy. All of these applications of community policing try to reduce crime by establishing linkages with neighborhood businesses, citizens, and social service agencies. Thus, law enforcement agencies become integral partners in improving the quality of life for the community.

Chief Reuben M. Greenberg, who was appointed Chief of Police in 1982, heads the police force in Charleston, South Carolina. His department strongly embraced community policing but created its own unique approach to the philosophy. The Charleston Police Department vigorously enforces the law and intentionally promotes the image of the police as a deterrent against crime. At the same time, the Department has established very close links to the community. For example, it is not uncommon for officers who walk beats to actively engage citizens in conversation about mundane matters. Chief Greenberg has demanded high ethics from his officers–for example, the use of profanity has been prohibited. An interesting element of Chief Greenberg's philosophy is the emphasis on victims' rights. Using this approach, the Department keeps close watch on known law breakers even after they have been released from the correctional system. A BOLO (Be on the Lookout) board was established in the Department that contained photos and personal information about offenders who might return to the community. When one of the perpetrators was identified in the community, the police would regularly question them about their activities.

The Charleston Police Department's model of combining vigorous law enforcement with community policing and the promotion of victims' rights, has been termed Victim Oriented Policing.

Definitions:

Community Oriented Policing: [A] form of policing oriented toward the public, or police forces' clients, and designed to provide communities with responsive, ethical, high-quality police service."[1]

Problem Oriented Policing: "A strategy to develop long-range plans to reduce recurrent crime and disorder problems... Requires the ability to analyze social problems, coordinate design solutions...and monitor the results of cooperative efforts."[2]

---

[1] Rush, George E. *The Dictionary of Criminal Justice*, 5th ed. New York, Dushkin/McGraw-Hill, 2000. Page 66.

CRITICAL THINKING: YOU DECIDE

Assume that a very strict version of victim-oriented policing becomes the predominant policing philosophy in the United States. However, in its new application, the registration of all formerly convicted criminals is required when they move into neighborhoods. This is a broadening of the current approach used by "Megan's Laws" jurisdictions. Is this new approach constitutionally sound? Is it a violation of due process?

_____

_____

_____

_____

_____

What arguments would you make to *justify* this new approach?

_____

_____

_____

_____

_____

_____

[2] Id, page 270.

ESSAY: ETHICS AND DISCRETION

Assume that you are a police officer with the Charleston Police Department. You are completely familiar with the entries on the BOLO board, and happen upon a recently-released convicted burglar. What should you do? Should you approach this person? To what extent should you engage him? Should you question him? If so, what questions would you ask?

_____

_____

_____

_____

_____

CASE OUTCOME

Community policing has become a national trend in the law enforcement community. Its application in Charleston, South Carolina is an interesting case study of a successful interpretation of the philosophy. The police in Charleston have had few injuries, their popularity in the community has risen dramatically, their use of force has decreased dramatically, and morale is high. Perhaps most importantly, the crime rate in Charleston has been consistently low.

ONLINE INVESTIGATION: THE INSIDE STORY

For an online search of these issues, students enter the keywords, "problem oriented policing," "community oriented policing," and "Chicago's Alternative Policing Strategy (CAPS)."

FYI: CAREER CONNECTION

For further information about community policing, visit the Web site of Policing.com at http://www.policing.com/.

For further information about the Charleston Police Department, visit their Web site at http://www.charleston-pd.org/.

Students should also contact the National Center for Community Policing.

CHAPTER 9: THE COURT SYSTEM AND ADJUDICATION PROCESS

CASE

Prosecutors are charged to represent the interests of the people and the state when conducting criminal proceedings against persons accused of committing criminal acts. When performing this charge, the prosecutor's duty is to review the case, file charges, evaluate available evidence, and use the evidence to prosecute the case to completion. This can be a labor-intensive and complicated progression of decisions that require choices to be made at every stage of the process. These decisions are at the heart of prosecutorial discretion, which is universally protected by law makers and judges, so long as the prosecutor does not abuse his or her discretion. In the performance of this discretion, the prosecutor will decide whether to bring charges against the accused, which charges should be filed, whether to bargain to drop or reduce charges; which evidence to present and how to present it, and what punishment to advocate against the accused. The law and local customs confer prosecutorial discretionary authority.

In Indiana, a woman was suspected of shooting her sons. She denied the allegation, but Indiana police believed that the suspect had a multiple personality disorder. The police asked an Indiana state prosecutor if they could hypnotize the defendant and question her. The prosecutor said that they could, they did so, and another personality named "Katie" admitted to committing the murders. The prosecutor then told the police that they had probable cause to arrest her for the crime. Confessions under hypnosis are not admissible in Indiana. The suspect continued to deny her culpability. Neither the prosecutor nor the officer told the judge at a probable cause hearing that the confession was elicited by hypnosis. She was arrested, charged with the murder, but the charges were later dropped when the hypnosis confession became known.

The accused then sued the prosecutor under 42 U.S.C. 1983 for violating her civil rights in an abuse of his discretion. The case was eventually heard by the U.S. Supreme Court as *Burns v. Reed*.

Definitions:

Prosecutorial discretion: Authority conferred on prosecuting attorneys to exercise his or her judgment in performing prosecutions on behalf of the people and the state.

CRITICAL THINKING: YOU DECIDE

Prosecutorial discretion is a significant center of authority in the overall law enforcement community. Because of the many available opportunities to exercise prosecutorial discretion, there are also many opportunities to abuse this discretion. How would you evaluate the parameters of a legitimate exercise of discretion? What is an abuse of discretion?

_____

_____

_____

_____

_____

_____

ESSAY: ETHICS AND DISCRETION

Assume that you are an Assistant District Attorney who has received a burglary case for prosecution. Your immediate superior, the Deputy District Attorney, tells you that she wants you to prosecute this case vigorously and to seek the maximum possible penalty against the accused. During your evaluation of the evidence, you discover that the burglary occurred in the home of the Deputy District Attorney's parents. You further discover that burglary prosecutions have never been a top priority for the Deputy D.A. You have also heard through the "grapevine" that your superior has expressed outrage that the accused broke into her parents' home and wants to see this person "put away" for as long as possible. Is the Deputy D.A.'s behavior ethical? Is it a legitimate exercise of prosecutorial discretion?

_____

_____

_____

_____

_____

If you suspect that she is abusing her discretionary authority, what should you do?

_____

_____

_____

_____

_____

_____

CASE OUTCOME

In *Burns v. Reed*, 500 U.S. 478 (1990), the Supreme Court ruled: "A state prosecuting attorney is absolutely immune from liability for damages under [42 U.S.C.] 1983 for participating in a probable cause hearing, but not for giving legal advice to the police."

ONLINE INVESTIGATION: THE INSIDE STORY

For an online search of prosecutorial discretion and prosecutors' offices, students should enter the keywords "United States Attorney," "attorney general," and "district attorney," to bring up Web sites and reports that discuss the duties and authority of prosecuting attorneys.

FYI: CAREER CONNECTION

For further information about prosecutors, access the National District Attorneys Association's Web page at http://www.ndaa.org/.

Students should also access the National Association of Attorneys' General Web page at http://www.naag.org/.

CHAPTER 10: COURTROOM PARTICIPANTS AND THE TRIAL

CASE

Criminal defense attorneys are often retained by clients who ask them to apply the most basic of defenses. For example, many clients will simply argue that the authorities have arrested the wrong man or woman. This kind of alibi defense makes the case that the defendant was unavailable to commit the crime. Defense attorneys are also retained by clients who have been confronted by the authorities with an overwhelming amount of evidence. In such cases, attorneys often conclude that the best defense may be to bargain with the prosecutor. In these circumstances, defendants make a plea for a lesser charge. Plea bargains have become a routine feature of the American criminal trial.

However, on occasion, defense counsels have clients who admittedly committed the acts for which they are being prosecuted, but whose circumstances require special consideration. "Battered woman syndrome" is one such circumstance.

Battered woman syndrome was identified and defined in 1979 when psychologist Dr. Lenore Walker reported findings based on her research of hundreds of cases of women who had been battered by their partners. In her book, *The Battered Woman*, Dr. Walker discussed several features of battered women syndrome. One feature is "learned helplessness" in which battered women learned that no matter what they might do, they could not stop the violence. Another feature is the "cycle of violence" in which battering occurs in three phases, including a tension-building phase, a battering phase, and a respite phase. A third feature is "hypervigilence" in which battered women are able to read the signs of danger quickly and accurately.

Some battered women have killed their partners, often during the tension-building phase, and used battered woman syndrome as a defense to charges of criminal homicide. In 1977, Francine Hughes was prosecuted for killing her husband. She had poured gasoline around his bed while he slept, and then ignited the fuel.

Definitions:

Alibi: "A type of defense…that proves the accused could not have committed the crime…since evidence offered shows the accused was in another place at the time the crime was committed."[1]

Criminal homicide: "The causing of the death of another person without legal justification or excuse."[2]

---

[1] Rush, George E. *The Dictionary of Criminal Justice*, 5th ed. New York: Dushkin/McGraw-Hill, 2000. Page 10.
[2] Id., page 90.

Defense Counsel: "Counsel for the defendant; an attorney who represents and aids the defendant."[3]

Plea Bargain: "[N]egotiation between prosecutor and defendant and/or his or her attorney, which often results in the defendant's entering of a guilty plea in exchange for the state's reduction of charges..."[4]

CRITICAL THINKING: YOU DECIDE

Assume the jury heard testimony confirming that Francine Hughes was a battered woman. Should this be a factor in the jury's deliberations? Why?

_____

_____

_____

_____

_____

_____

_____

---

[3] Id, page 102.
[4] Id., page 252.

If the jury also heard testimony indicating Francine Hughes feared for her life, what kind of defenses might be raised by the defense team? Which defenses do you think would be most persuasive to the jury?

_____

_____

_____

_____

_____

_____

What other considerations should be discussed during the jury's deliberations?

_____

_____

_____

_____

_____

_____

ESSAY: ETHICS AND DISCRETION

Assume that courtroom testimony in a murder trial shows that a defendant indeed exhibits the features of learned helplessness, cycles of violence, and hypervigilence. Also assume that this is a jurisdiction where the battered woman syndrome defense has been used successfully.

What should the prosecutor do? Should he or she continue with the prosecution? Modify the charges? Perhaps even drop the charges?

_____

_____

_____

_____

_____

_____

_____

CASE OUTCOME

The Francine Hughes case was tried at a time before battered woman syndrome was recognized and accepted and before battered person defenses succeeded as exclusive defenses. In November 1977, Francine Hughes was acquitted. Her defense was based on temporary insanity. The case was dramatized by the 1984 television film, "The Burning Bed."

ONLINE INVESTIGATION: THE INSIDE STORY

For a general online search, students should enter the keywords, "Battered Woman Syndrome," "Francine Hughes," or "burning bed case" to bring up Web sites and reports that discuss the case. For legal analysis of battered woman syndrome, students should access Lexis-Nexis Academic Universe.

FYI: CAREER CONNECTION

This case involved professionals from the private sector who work within the criminal justice system. In this case, these professionals included defense counsel and psychologists.

For further information about forensic psychology, access the American Board of Forensic Psychology's Web site at http://www.abfp.com/.

For further information about criminal defense work, access the Web site of the Criminal Justice Section of the American Bar Association's at http://www.abanet.org/crimjust/.

CHAPTER 11: SENTENCING AND SANCTIONS

CASE

Judges sit as the "trier of law" in criminal trials. Their duty is to judge whether evidence is presented in a constitutional manner, assure that the constitutional rights of all participants are protected, and to maintain a high standard of decorum and order during the trial. Within the framework of this overarching duty, judges have the discretion to rule upon a range of procedural and legal questions that frequently arise during the trial. The exercise of judicial discretion generally arises when the court must decide on issues such as appropriate bail, whether to accept or reject pleas, rule on motions to dismiss, impose sentences, or revoke probation. Discretionary authority is conferred by law.

In Houston, Texas, a thirty-seven-year-old mother was arrested on June 20, 2001 and charged with the murder of her five children. Andrea Pia Yates confessed to drowning all five children in a bathtub. The trial was held in a state district court presided over by Judge Belinda Hill. During the trial, Yates' defense counsel introduced evidence and expert testimony to support their defense that she was legally insane–arguing that she was not guilty by reason of insanity. If successful, this defense would have precluded her conviction for crimes that could have led to a death sentence. The defense successfully introduced evidence that Yates had been diagnosed with severe depression and schizophrenia. However, the jury concluded that she knew right from wrong at the time of the killings, and so she was therefore not legally insane. They convicted her of a capital crime.

Judge Hill received the jury's decision. During the pre-sentencing phase, the prosecutor did not vigorously pursue a recommendation in favor of executing Yates, and the jury recommended to the court that she be given a life sentence.

Definitions:

Judicial discretion: Authority conferred by law on a court that allows the court to act in accordance with its reasoning.

Trier of law: The court. Its duty is to preside over criminal proceedings and assure that constitutional protections and requirements are upheld.

CRITICAL THINKING: YOU DECIDE

Depending on the laws of particular jurisdictions, the pre-sentencing phase of a trial is one in which the judge exercises his or her discretion over the fate of the accused. Does it make sense to permit this kind of discretion to reside with judges? Should it reside with the jury?

_____

_____

_____

_____

_____

Absent a showing of an abuse of discretion, the judge's decision will stand. Is this fair? How broadly should "abuse of discretion" be defined?

_____

_____

_____

_____

_____

ESSAY: ETHICS AND DISCRETION

Assume that you are a criminal trial judge presiding over a trial with issues similar to the Yates trial. Assume further that the jury recommended that the accused be sentenced the maximum possible penalty. How would you rule on the jury's recommendation?

_____

_____

_____

_____

_____

_____

To what extent should the evidence regarding the defendant's mental condition affect your decision?

_____

_____

_____

_____

_____

_____

CASE OUTCOME

Judge Hill, in her discretion, had the authority to deny the jury's recommendation and could have sentenced Yates to death. However, the judge accepted the recommendation, ruling that Yates receive a life sentence and psychiatric treatment. Under this ruling, the defendant would not be eligible for parole for the next forty years.

ONLINE INVESTIGATION: THE INSIDE STORY

For an online search of judicial discretion, students should enter the keywords, "sentencing guidelines" and "insanity defense," to bring up Web sites and reports that discuss sentencing issues and the parameters for using the insanity defense.

FYI: CAREER CONNECTION

For further information about judges and the courts, access the Federal Judiciary Web page at http://www.uscourts.gov/.

Students should also access the Judicial Conference's Web page for their home states.

CHAPTER 12: JAILS AND PRISONS

CASE

"Prisoners' rights" is a concept that is often at the center of policy and political debates. The basic standard for determining the rights of prisoners is a "balancing test" that balances their rights against the legitimate needs for prison security, custody, and safety. The underlying concept is that inmates' rights are conditional rights that are regulated and can be taken away, if necessary.

Having said this, prisoners do have the right to be provided with the basic necessities for health and survival. Prison administrators cannot engage in deliberate indifference to inmate health. There is a general requirement to provide inmates with a healthy environment, including the provision of food, clothing, and shelter. Included in this general requirement is the provision of adequate medical care.

Outbreaks of disease in prisons have been of concern to prison administrators since the beginning of the American model of corrections. In the modern era, the incidence of HIV-AIDS has become a serious concern in prisons and jails. AIDS is the leading cause of death among inmates, and from 1991 to 1996, AIDS caused one out of every three state prison deaths. As of 1997, New York state and Florida had the highest and second-highest incidence, respectively, of AIDS among inmates.

Considering the rising incidence of AIDS in society in general, it should be no surprise that the disease is prevalent in prisons. From a law enforcement policy perspective, reducing the incidence of AIDS in the correctional system should be a top priority. The danger is that an epidemic of AIDS in the nation's prisons would strain law enforcement resources, especially the prison healthcare system. Another danger is a general societal danger that is simply stated–most inmates will someday be returned to society. Thus, HIV-positive returnees would pose a medical problem for the broader society.

Definitions:

AIDS: Acquired Immunodeficiency Syndrome.

HIV: Human Immunodeficiency Virus.

CRITICAL THINKING: YOU DECIDE

HIV-AIDS is a serious concern in the American correctional system. Accurate data on the true incidence of HIV is always needed. Assume that you are a law enforcement researcher working on a national effort to collect this information. How would you obtain these data? What kinds of data-gathering programs would you recommend to state and local corrections administrators?

_____

_____

_____

_____

_____

_____

Who is best qualified to conduct this kind of data-gathering at the state and local levels?

_____

_____

_____

_____

_____

_____

ESSAY: ETHICS AND DISCRETION

Assume that you are a prison administrator and that you have recently conducted a thorough audit of the inmate population for HIV. The findings of the audit are not good; there is a high incidence of HIV and AIDS. How can you protect prison staff? How can you protect the other inmates?

_____

_____

_____

_____

_____

What should be done with the HIV-positive population? What kind of support would you request from the correctional system's top administrators?

_____

_____

_____

_____

_____

CASE OUTCOME

Testing for HIV-AIDS has increased in the correctional system. Nevertheless, the problem is not one that is widely known outside of the law enforcement profession. The public health ramifications of HIV in prison have not been widely debated outside of academic and practitioner groups.

ONLINE INVESTIGATION: THE INSIDE STORY

For an online search of medical and other issues in the nation's prisons, students should enter the keywords, "prisoners' rights," "prison conditions," and "inmates' rights."

FYI: CAREER CONNECTION

For information about careers in corrections, access the Web pages of the state correctional officers' association in your state.

Students should also access the Web site of the American Correctional Association at http://www.corrections.com/aca/.

CHAPTER 13: PROBATION AND PAROLE

CASE

The search for innovative treatment alternatives has led many jurisdictions to develop strict diversion programs. "Shock" programs have become popular as innovative treatment alternatives used to divert juveniles away from detention. These are intended to radically change juvenile behavior. Shock intervention comes at a critical moment in the juvenile's life, with the purpose of changing juvenile behavior.

Boot camps are a popular application of shock program theory. Boot camps are usually used for first-time, non-violent offenders. Boot camp cycles often last for six months. The program can be quite intensive, and often only one-half of juveniles complete the course. The common characteristic of boot camps is military-style regimentation. Participants are given military-style haircuts and wear uniforms. Strict rules are imposed, emphasizing respect for and obedience to authority. Permission must be given to speak, eat, and engage in other personal activities. Punishment is swift and usually involves some sort of physical exercise. The daily regimen might also include six to eight hours of labor such as community service. Trained law enforcement officers who use military-style drill instructor methods directly supervise participants.

Another shock program is the "scared straight" programs. Scared straight programs expose juvenile offenders to the realities of adult prison life. Prison inmates serving long sentences volunteer to graphically lecture juveniles about everyday life in prison, emphasizing what happens to young newcomers in prison. The language is explicit, and the confrontations are intensive. The purpose of scared straight programs is to use fear as intensive treatment intervention. The scared straight approach was popularized in 1979 by the film, *Scared Straight*, which was a documentary about seventeen juvenile delinquents in New Jersey who participated in the program. Participants were sent to Rahway Prison, now called East Jersey State Prison, and were confronted by hardened convicts who were participating in the prison's Lifers' Program.

Definitions:

Boot camps: Military-style intervention programs that divert offenders out of the system and into a regimented regime intended to discipline them and modify their behavior.

"Scared straight" programs: Intervention programs that divert offenders out of the system and into a day-long intensive session with hardened criminals intended to use fear to modify their behavior.

"Shock" programs: Programs that provide intensive intervention to participants with the goal of radically changing their behavior.

CRITICAL THINKING: YOU DECIDE

Assume that you are a social worker for a juvenile justice agency. One of your cases involves an offender who is in trouble with the authorities for the first time. He has been in trouble in school, but this is the first time he has been declared a juvenile delinquent. Why might you recommend that he enroll in a shock treatment program?

_____

_____

_____

_____

_____

_____

What factors would you consider for your recommendation?

_____

_____

_____

_____

_____

_____

ESSAY: ETHICS AND DISCRETION

Assume that you are a juvenile justice officer investigating a case on behalf of the juvenile court. The juvenile court has just begun experimenting with shock programs. No data exists yet for whether these programs work in your state. What factors would you weigh prior to making your recommendation to the court?

_____

_____

_____

_____

_____

Why might you rule _against_ using shock intervention for the first time?

_____

_____

_____

_____

_____

_____

CASE OUTCOME

The effectiveness of boot camps is uncertain. These seem to work for some participants but not work for others; some become productive, and others become recidivists. However, the juvenile and criminal justice systems continue to invest resources into boot camp programs, in part because these are cheaper than incarceration in detention facilities and prisons. Of the original Rahway Prison cohort, most participants eventually led productive lives, although a few did have problems later in life.

ONLINE INVESTIGATION: THE INSIDE STORY

For an online search of shock intervention, students should enter the keywords, "boot camps" and "scared straight," to bring up Web sites and reports discussing these programs.

FYI: CAREER CONNECTION

For information about careers in probation and how shock programs might be used as alternatives, access the Web page of the state probation and parole officers' associations in your state.

Students should also access the Web site of the American Probation and Parole Association at http://www.appa-net.org/.

CHAPTER 14: PREVENTION AND CORRECTION IN THE COMMUNITY

CASE

Criminal justice in the United States is fairly efficient in its processing of criminal suspects through the system. The police, courts, and corrections components of the system tend to be professional and capable mechanisms of social control. However, post-release supervision of criminals is a constantly evolving process that uses technological advances to monitor people. There have certainly been new innovations in post-release supervision that are brought about by social and political concerns, but one case in particular changed the consciousness of communities and law enforcement officials around the country.

In 1994, a terrible crime occurred in Hamilton Township, New Jersey. A young girl, seven-year-old Megan Kanka, was raped and murdered by Jesse K. Temmendequas, who lived across the street from her. The distinguishing elements of this case were twofold: First, Temmendequas was a twice-convicted child molester who had been released from the corrections system; second, none of the residents of the neighborhood where he lived knew about his background. At that time, no state required the notification of community residents when a released criminal moved into a neighborhood, so Temmendequas lived anonymously until he murdered a young girl.

A public outcry demanded that the criminal justice system address the problem of post-release sex offenders living in neighborhoods without the knowledge of residents. The outcome was the passage of "Megan's Laws" throughout the United States. Megan's Laws mandate that communities be notified when released sex offenders move into neighborhoods. These also require the released offenders to register with local police departments when they take up a new residence. In 1994, New Jersey became the first state to pass a Megan's Law; within a short period of time, all fifty states had passed some type of Megan's Law. As a matter of policy, Megan's Laws are now a regular feature of the American criminal justice system. Politically, these laws are very popular.

Definitions:

Megan's Laws: "A control strategy...mandating notification to a community when a convicted sex offender moves in, with different levels of notification required for different levels of offense."[1]

---

[1] Rush, George E. *The Dictionary of Criminal Justice*, 5th ed. New York: Dushkin/McGraw-Hill, 2000. Page 210.

CRITICAL THINKING: YOU DECIDE

Persons who are convicted of crimes and serve their sentence have, in theory, "repaid their debt to society." Their trials, convictions, and sentences are a kind of value-judgment of the seriousness of their offenses. When the requirements of that value-judgment are satisfied, should that person not be allowed to re-enter society? Should that person not be allowed to re-enter *anonymously* if they so desire?

_____

_____

_____

_____

_____

_____

For what other criminal offenses, should the state impose requirements of registration and notification? What are the constitutional issues that arise from this policy?

_____

_____

_____

_____

_____

_____

ESSAY: ETHICS AND DISCRETION

Assume that you are a parole officer who has former a client that is being monitored under a Megan's Law. He appears to be fully rehabilitated, has been married, and is now raising a family. You find out that he has moved away to a new town, and has failed to register. He has told you that he simply wants a "fresh start" so that he can raise his family in peace. What should you do?

_____

_____

_____

_____

_____

_____

CASE OUTCOME

Federal courts have upheld the basic provisions of Megan's Laws. California led the trend to enhance registration by distributing a CD-ROM with the names of more than 60,000 sex offenders living in the state. Pennsylvania's law is typical of strongly-worded laws. In Pennsylvania, enhanced restrictions and stronger possible penalties will be applied for failure to register, so long as the state has met its burden to show that the person is a "sexually violent predator."

ONLINE INVESTIGATION: THE INSIDE STORY

For a general online search, students should enter the keywords, "Megan's Laws" and "Megan Kanka," to bring up Web sites and reports that discuss the case and Megan's Laws.

FYI: CAREER CONNECTION

For information about careers in parole, access the Web page of the state probation and parole officers' association in your state.

Students should also access the Web site of the American Probation and Parole Association at http://www.appa-net.org/.

CHAPTER 15: CHALLENGES IN THE CRIMINAL JUSTICE SYSTEM

CASE

The term, "New Terrorism," has been applied to the modern terrorist environment as a way to distinguish it from terrorist environments of the recent past. In the past, terrorist movements had several general features: They were mostly secular, they were organized hierarchically, they had state benefactors, their choice of targets was discriminating, and they used conventional weapons. In the modern terrorist environment, many terrorists have developed a new profile: They are sectarian (that is, religious), they are organized "horizontally" as small independent cells, they are often financially independent, their choice of targets is indiscriminate, and their potential use of weapons of mass destruction is a real threat.

One group, al Qaeda ("the Base"), is a representative case study of the New Terrorism. It is a loose network of Islamic revolutionaries that is organized in autonomous cells scattered as "sleepers" around the globe. Sleepers ward off suspicion by integrating themselves into their host countries and then become active when called upon–this process often takes place over a period of years. Osama bin Laden is a wealthy Saudi Arabian heir to a construction company fortune who is the mastermind behind al Qaeda. Under his guidance, the group became financially independent from state sponsorship, and their agenda was developed to spread holy war and drive Western influences out of Muslim countries.

Al Qaeda's financial empire has received a great deal of attention from law enforcement and security officials, and electronic technologies have been used to penetrate its holdings. Agencies were tracking al Qaeda's finances before the attacks of September 11, 2001 in response to the terrorist bombings of the U.S. embassies in Kenya and Tanzania. Al Qaeda's money flow has been tracked using satellites via the ultra-secret National Security Agency, which can monitor and intercept banking transfers. Accounts can be deleted, changed, transferred, or otherwise disrupted–done remotely and electronically.

Definitions:

Al Qaeda: A loose network of radical Islamic revolutionaries, originally founded by Osama bin Laden.

New Terrorism: A terrorist environment that is largely sectarian and these are organized into small independent cells. These cells will potentially use weapons of mass destruction if they can obtain these.

CRITICAL THINKING: YOU DECIDE

Assume that you are a special agent for the Federal Bureau of Investigation assigned to a counter-terrorism investigation unit. Assume also that you have information that an international terrorist group has set up a fund-raising "front" in a major urban area. It poses as a charity foundation, but you have information that it is transferring funds into accounts that are accessed by a terrorist group calling itself the Northern Ireland Liberation Movement. What factors will you weigh in making a recommendation about whether to monitor the account?

_____

_____

_____

_____

_____

_____

What factors would you need to recommend a covert electronic operation to disrupt the account?

_____

_____

_____

_____

_____

Under what conditions would you allow the account to remain active for the time being?

_____

_____

_____

_____

_____

_____

ESSAY: ETHICS AND DISCRETION

Assume that you are the same special agent with the same assignment discussed above. You have discovered credible evidence that a terrorist cell is operating in a major city, but do not know who they are or where they are. Your have a profile–a "terrorist profile"–of their nationality and age. What is your recommendation for electronic surveillance?

_____

_____

_____

_____

What portion of the population should be "bugged?" Should you attempt to monitor all people in the urban area who fit the terrorist profile?

_____

_____

_____

_____

_____

_____

_____

CASE OUTCOME

Electronic surveillance and disruption of terrorist financial networks is an international endeavor. It requires government agencies to covertly monitor individuals and accounts, and to collect intelligence both at home and abroad. Law enforcement agencies must, out of necessity, work in cooperation with intelligence agencies. Managing the balance between practical necessity and constitutional protections can be a complicated process.

ONLINE INVESTIGATION: THE INSIDE STORY

For an online search of electronic surveillance and issues pertaining to the investigation of terrorism, students should enter the keywords, "National Security Agency," "Central Intelligence Agency," and "Federal Bureau of Investigation."

FYI: CAREER CONNECTION

For information about careers in counter-terrorism, access the web pages of the FBI, CIA, NSA , and U.S. Department of State.

http://www.fbi.gov.
http://www.cia.gov.
http://www.nsa.gov.
http://www.state.gov.

CHAPTER ONE

1.1   Who said the cornerstone of civilization is the belief that "our fellowman will abide by the Law?"
a. Clarence Thomas
b. Thomas Jefferson
c. Roscoe Pound
d. Thurgood Marshall

1.2   What tactic did Dr. Martin Luther King promote during the civil rights struggle of the 1960's?
a. Rioting
b. Civil Disobedience
c. Ethnic Cleansing
d. Law Suits

1.3   What school expelled Autherine Lucy in 1956?
a. University of Alabama
b. North Carolina State University
c. University of California
d. City University of New York

1.4   In what year was Megar Evers murdered?
a. 1959
b. 1960
c. 1961
d. 1962

1.5   Which president declared a "war on crime?"
a. Nixon
b. Kennedy
c. Ford
d. Johnson

1.6   In what year was the Omnibus Crime Control and Safe Streets Act passed?
a. 1968
b. 1969
c. 1970
d. 1971

1.7 In the late 1960's, which federal program acted as a conduit for federal funds to state and local law enforcement agencies?
a. Law Enforcement Educational Program
b. Law Enforcement Achievement Program
c. Law Enforcement Assistance Administration
d. Law Enforcement Education Administration

1.8 How many Japanese Americans were moved to detention centers during WWII?
a. 1 million
b. 120,000
c. 50,000
d. 250,000

1.9 Who heads the Office of Homeland Security?
a. Tom Ridge
b. Bob Dole
c. Joe McCarthy
d. Richard Clarke

1.10 Which president created the post of National Coordinator for Security?
a. Clinton
b. Bush
c. Carter
d. Johnson

1.11 Who argued that all humans are endowed with "natural rights?"
a. Jeremy Bentham
b. Cesare Beccara
c. Thomas Hobbes
d. John Locke

1.12 In what year was the Bill of Rights added to the Constitution?
a. 1778
b. 1782
c. 1791
d. 1801

1.13 Who declared "justice is not the will of the majority or of the wealthier, but the course of action which the moral aim of the state requires?"
a. Plato
b. Hobbes
c. Aristotle
d. Locke

1.14   Which is an example of bioterrorism?
        a. Dropping an atomic bomb.
        b. Placing salmonella in the water supply of a city.
        c. Using a computer program to shut down a power grid.
        d. None of the above are examples of bioterrorism.

1.15   The organized use of violence with the aim of promoting political or social change is
        called:
        a. Civil disobedience
        b. Guerilla warfare
        c. Revolution
        d. Terrorism

1.16   The terrorist group F.A.L.N originated in what country?
        a. Puerto Rico
        b. Mexico
        c. Panama
        d. Costa Rica

1.17   Which below is not one of the three acts of domestic terrorism most often encountered by
        local and state police?
        a. Act of violence committed by militias and extremist groups or individuals.
        b. Hackers using computer technology to disrupt society.
        c. Violence against abortion clinics and personnel.
        d. Ecoterrorism

1.18   What terrorist group focuses its actions upon "liberating" animals used in scientific
        experiments?
        a. KKK
        b. ELF
        c. ALF
        d. PETA

1.19   Who said criminology is "the body of knowledge regarding crime as a social
        phenomenon?"
        a. Edwin Sutherland
        b. Raffaele Garofalo
        c. Emile Durkheim
        d. Sigmund Freud

1.20   In what country can a prosecutor drop criminal charges against a defendant if he
        apologizes to the victim?
        a. France
        b. Thailand
        c. Japan
        d. Bermuda

1.21   How many judges hear criminal cases in Japan?
        a. Two
        b. Three
        c. Four
        d. None. Japan uses a jury system.

1.22   What is counter terrorism?
        a. The use of biological weapons to change political views.
        b. The response to terrorism and the efforts to stop it.
        c. The fear of terrorism brought on by media reports.
        d. None of the above.

1.23   In what country was Lori Berenson convicted and sentenced to life imprisonment without
        benefit of a trial?
        a. Peru
        b. Mexico
        c. Columbia
        d. Belize

1.24   In what year did the FBI open the Strategic Information and Operations Center?
        a. 1985
        b. 1990
        c. 1998
        d. 2001

1.25   Which below is an example of an informal sanction?
        a. Imprisonment
        b. Fines
        c. Torts
        d. Parental disapproval

CHAPTER TWO

2.1   Which is not a source of official crime statistics?
    a. Bureau of Justice Statistics
    b. Federal Bureau of Investigation
    c. National Crime Victimization Survey
    d. National Criminal Justice Reference Service

2.2   When did Cleveland, OH perform its first crime survey?
    a. 1920's
    b. 1900
    c. 1930's
    d. 1940's

2.3   The Uniform Crime Report is prepared by:
    a. The Bureau of Justice Statistics
    b. The National Criminal Justice Reference Service
    c. Interpol
    d. The Federal Bureau of Investigation

2.4   What does the "crime clock" do?
    a. Reports how often a crime is solved.
    b. Reports how often a crime is committed.
    c. Reports how often a crime is prosecuted.
    d. None of the above.

2.5   The rule of counting only the most serious crime in incidents with multiple crimes was
    called:
    a. The heinousness rule.
    b. The violence rule.
    c. The hierarchy rule.
    d. The statistical rule.

2.6   What part of the UCR is used to report serious crimes?
    a. Part I
    b. Part II
    c. Part III
    d. Part IV

2.7   Which below is not an Index Crime?
    a. Larceny
    b. Arson
    c. Drug dealing
    d. Motor vehicle theft

2.8   In what year was the National Crime Victim Survey first used?
        a. 1970
        b. 1972
        c. 1974
        d. 1976

2.9   In what year was the Hate Crime Statistics Act passed?
        a. 1990
        b. 1980
        c. 1970
        d. 1960

2.10   Your chance of being victimized by theft ranks third behind:
        a. Your chance of being murdered or raped.
        b. Your chance of being injured accidentally either at home or otherwise.
        c. Your chance of being robbed or getting cancer.
        d. None of the above.

2.11   What analogy of the criminal justice system implies that each political entity is separate
        and that there is a hierarchy with local political entities at the bottom and the Federal
        government at the top?
        a. Picket fence
        b. Figure eight
        c. Wedding cake
        d. Domino

2.12   The model of criminal justice that emphasizes efficient and effective justice is known as:
        a. The crime control model
        b. The retribution model
        c. The due process model
        d. The rehabilitation model

2.13   The basic source of due process rights is:
        a. The U.S. Constitution
        b. State statutes
        c. The Bill of Rights
        d. Both a and c.

2.14   Generally speaking, at what age would a defendant move from the jurisdiction of the
        juvenile courts to the jurisdiction of adult criminal court?
        a. 14
        b. 16
        c. 18
        d. 21

2.15   Which below is not a status offense?
       a. Drinking
       b. Smoking
       c. Vandalism
       d. Sexual activity

2.16   In what year was the age of maturity originally set at 18 years?
       a. 1899
       b. 1888
       c. 1877
       d. 1866

2.17   What state executed a 12 year old girl in 1786?
       a. Mississippi
       b. Connecticut
       c. Ohio
       d. Texas

2.18   Which below is an example of "diversion"?
       a. Community Service
       b. Parole
       c. Imprisonment
       d. Death Penalty

2.19   The two primary agencies involved in international crime are:
       a. The FBI and CIA
       b. The London Metropolitan Police and the U.N.
       c. The BATF and Interpol
       d. The U.N. and Interpol

2.20   In what year was Interpol formed?
       a. 1890
       b. 1900
       c. 1914
       d. 1920

2.21   The concept that requires that the police must have evidence in order to make an arrest is
       called:
       a. Probable cause
       b. Due process
       c. Powers of arrest
       d. Policies and procedures

2.22   After someone has been arrested, how many hours may they be held before being
        formally charged or released?
        a.   72
        b.   48
        c.   36
        d.   24

2.23   The preliminary hearing is also known as:
        a.   The first appearance.
        b.   Booking
        c.   The probable cause hearing.
        d.   None of the above.

2.24   A formal, written legal document forwarded to the court, asserting that there is probable
        cause too believe that the defendant committed an offense is called:
        a.   An indictment
        b.   An arraignment
        c.   An appeal
        d.   A motion

2.25   Early release from prison before the maximum sentence is served, based on evidence of
        rehabilitation and good behavior of the inmate is called:
        a.   Probation
        b.   Parole
        c.   Clemency
        d.   Pardon

CHAPTER THREE

3.1   Who argued that humans, if left to their own nature, would naturally tend toward bad behaviors?
        a. Machiavelli
        b. Hobbes
        c. Golding
        d. Locke

3.2   What was the major source of criminal law during the Middle Ages?
        a. The King's court
        b. The Catholic Church
        c. Village counsels
        d. None of the above.

3.3   In what year did the Salem Witchcraft trials take place?
        a. 1650
        b. 1666
        c. 1692
        d. 1702

3.4   The breaching of a social norm is called:
        a. Crime
        b. Anti-social behavior
        c. Individualism
        d. Deviance

3.5   A detailed examination of a specific person or crime is known as a:
        a. Theory
        b. Case study
        c. Investigation
        d. Both a and c are correct.

3.6   A general theory is also known as a:
        a. Macro theory
        b. Middle range theory
        c. Wide range theory
        d. Narrow theory

3.7   Who founded the classical school of criminology?
        a. Locke
        b. Hobbes
        c. Bentham
        d. Beccaria

3.8   In what year was Becaria's *Dei delitti e Delle Pene* published in Italy?
   a. 1760
   b. 1762
   c. 1764
   d. 1768

3.9   Who founded the neoclassical school of criminology?
   a. Locke
   b. Hobbes
   c. Bentham
   e. Beccaria

3.10   Who created the felicitic calculus?
   a. Bentham
   b. Hobbes
   c. Beccaria
   d. Locke

3.11   One of the early proponents of determinism was:
   a. Gulick
   b. Gall
   c. Southerland
   d. Freud

3.12   Who studied the Jukes family?
   a. Kallikak
   b. Goddard
   c. Dugdale
   d. Darwin

3.13   The study of the physical traits of criminals was called:
   a. Atavistic theorem
   b. Phrenology
   c. Atavistic criminology
   d. Atavistic stigmata

3.14   Which below is not one of Lombroso's three types of criminals?
   a. Made criminal
   b. Born criminal
   c. Insane criminal
   d. Occasional criminal

3.15   What theory is based on the assumption that there is a link between the mind and the body and that this link is expressed in the body type of an individual.
       a. Biological theory
       b. XYY Chromosome theory
       c. Somatotype theory
       d. Evolutionary theory

3.16   Males account for what percentage of all convicted criminals?
       a. 50%
       b. 90%
       c. 85%
       d. 40%

3.17   The primary control center for the fear response in the human brain is the:
       a. Autonomic nervous system
       b. Sympathetic nervous system
       c. Central nervous system
       d. Pituitary gland

3.18   Who developed the criminal personality theory?
       a. Gall and Kant
       b. Southerland
       c. Freud
       d. Yochelson and Samenow

3.19   What theory says that society - not free will, biology, or psychology - determines criminal behavior?
       a. Classical theory
       b. Social determinism
       c. Psychological theory
       d. Biological theory

3.20   A feeling of "normlessness" is known as:
       a. Ennui
       b. Anomie
       c. Social dysfunction
       d. Social unrest

3.21   What theory did Shaw, McKay and Burgess develop?
       a. Zone theory
       b. Social disorganization theory
       c. Social determinism
       d. Differential association theory

3.22   Which below is not an example of atavistic stigmata?
        a. Beetle brow
        b. Fair skin
        c. Excessive body hair
        d. Sloping forehead

3.23   What theory assumes that people are law-abiding but will resort to crime when they are
        frustrated in finding legitimate means to economic success?
        a. Labeling theory
        b. Differential opportunity theory
        c. Strain theory
        d. Cultural deviance theory

3.24   Who advocated a violent overthrow of the ruling class as a way to end crime?
        a. Marx
        b. Quinney
        c. Adler
        d. Simon

3.25   What theory says that crime can be prevented through environmental design?
        a. Conflict theory
        b. Crime prevention through environmental design
        c. Containment theory
        d. Classical criminology

CHAPTER FOUR

4.1   When did King Henry VIII proclaim himself the head of the Church of England?
a. 1530
b. 1534
c. 1542
d. 1557

4.2   What declares that the standards of behavior and privilege are not established by kings or religious leaders, but by rules and procedures that define and prohibit certain behaviors as illegal or criminal and prescribe punishments for those behaviors?
a. Rule of law
b. Divine right
c. Justice
d. Due process

4.3   Which crime is *mala in se*?
a. Parking violations
b. Underage drinking
c. Traffic infractions
d. Rape

4.4   If you strike someone, you have committed the crime of?
a. Robbery
b. Theft
c. Assault
d. Conspiracy

4.5   Where did the common law originate?
a. England
b. France
c. Spain
d. Italy

4.6   What was the punishment for theft in colonial New Haven, Conn?
a. Forced labor
b. Whipping
c. Public humiliation
d. Death

4.7   When did the term "blue laws" first appear in writing?
       a. 1710
       b. 1791
       c. 1748
       d. 1762

4.8   Which below is a felony crime?
       a. Rape
       b. Murder
       c. Arson
       d. All the above are felony crimes.

4.9   What legal principle requires that laws must be made public before they can be enforced?
       a. Principle of legality
       b. Due process
       c. Ex post facto
       d. Void for overbreadth

4.10   "Ex post facto" means:
       a. Before the fact.
       b. Beside the fact.
       c. Not after the fact.
       d. Not factual.

4.11   What requires the government to follow established procedures in carrying out the law
       and to treat defendants in a criminal trial equally?
       a. Substantive due process
       b. Procedural due process
       c. Neither of the above.
       d. Both of the above.

4.12   The law of precedent is also known as:
       a. Stare decisis
       b. Judicial review
       c. Due process
       d. Continental system

4.13   Which Amendment to the U.S. Constitution is not concerned with the right to privacy?
       a. First Amendment
       b. Second Amendment
       c. Fourth Amendment
       d. Ninth Amendment

4.14   Which below is an example of *actus reus*?
        a. Thinking about killing your spouse.
        b. Daydreaming about pulling off the perfect theft.
        c. Buying a gun to use in a robbery.
        d. Joking with a friend about stealing something.

4.15   Which below is not one of the four different states of "guilty mind" that can be applied to
        an action?
        a. General intent
        b. Specific intent
        c. Constructive intent
        d. All above are examples of "guilty mind."

4.16   Which below isn't an example of an inchoate offense?
        a. Solicitation
        b. Theft
        c. Conspiracy
        d. Attempt

4.17   How many people are required for a conspiracy?
        a. Two or more.
        b. Three or more.
        c. One.
        d. Four or more.

4.18   If the perpetrator of a crime says that the victim of that crime actively participated in the
        behavior that led to his injury, he is using the defense of:
        a. Alibi
        b. Immunity
        c. Mistake
        d. Consent

4.19   If a diplomatic officer gets caught speeding, the special protection against prosecution he
        enjoys is called:
        a. Necessity
        b. Entrapment
        c. Immunity
        d. Alibi

4.20   If someone attacks you physically, and in defending yourself you kill your attacker, what
        defense would you claim?
        a. Self defense
        b. Duress
        c. Necessity
        d. Ignorance or Mistake of the law

4.21   Who did Daniel M'Naghten intend to kill?
        a. Winston Churchill
        b. Robert Peel
        c. Edward Drummond
        d. No one.

4.22   The crime is the failure to act or the lack of action rather than the commission of an illegal act.
        a. Constructive intent
        b. *Actus Reus*
        c. Crimes of omission
        d. Concurrence

4.23   The term "corpus delicti" means:
        a. The dead body at the crime scene.
        b. The elements that make up a crime.
        c. Both a and b.
        d. Neither a or b.

4.24   In the Middle Ages, rape was a crime against:
        a. Property
        b. Women
        c. The state
        d. The church

4.25   If someone pulls a gun on you and demands that you give them all the money you have in your wallet, they have committed the crime of:
        a. Burglary
        b. Theft
        c. Robbery
        d. Assault

CHAPTER FIVE

5.1   The body of laws that directs how the criminal justice system operates at each stage of
       the process is called:
       a. Rules of evidence
       b. Procedural law
       c. Policies and procedures
       d. Constitutional law

5.2   What stipulates the requirements for introducing evidence and defines the qualifications
       of an expert witness and the nature of the testimony he or she may give?
       a. Rules of evidence
       b. Procedural law
       c. Policies and procedures
       d. Constitutional law

5.3   The exclusionary rule traces to what landmark case?
       a. Miranda v. Arizona
       b. Silverthorn Lumber Company v. U.S.
       c. Weeks v United States
       d. Mapp v. Ohio

5.4   What Amendment to the U.S. Constitution states "The right of the people to be secure in
       their persons, houses, papers, and effects, against unreasonable searches and seizures,
       shall not be violated, and no warrants shall issue, but upon probable cause..."
       a. First Amendment
       b. Second Amendment
       c. Third Amendment
       d. Fourth Amendment

5.5   In what landmark case did the Supreme Court say that evidence in the plain view of
       officers is admissible in court?
       a. Harris v. U.S.
       b. Mapp v. Ohio
       c. Wolf v. Colorado
       d. Weeks v. United States

5.6   What doctrine says that evidence obtained in the search of an automobile without a
        warrant is admissible in court if the officer has probable cause to believe that a crime has
        occurred and the circumstances are such that the delay in searching the automobile would
        result in the loss of evidence?
        a. The Thomas Doctrine
        b. The Carroll Doctrine
        c. The Davis Doctrine
        d. The Aadams Doctrine

5.7   What did the term "ground zero" refer to prior to September 11, 2001?
        a. The site of the bomb blast in Oklahoma City.
        b. Hiroshima
        c. Racial profiling in New Jersey
        d. None of the above.

5.8   Civil suits against federal law enforcement agents for denial of constitutional rights are
        called:
        a. Bivens actions
        b. Carroll actions
        c. Warren actions
        d. King actions

5.9   The pat down doctrine originated with what landmark case?
        a. Mapp v. Ohio
        b. Miranda v. Arizona
        c. Terry v. Ohio
        d. All of the above.

5.10   The fleeing felon doctrine was deemed unconstitutional in what year?
        a. 1980
        b. 1985
        c. 1976
        d. 1972

5.11   When a police officer draws and/or fires his weapon he is using:
        a. Reasonable force
        b. Unreasonable force
        c. Deadly force
        d. Aggravating force

5.12   What doctrine prohibits the use of evidence or testimony obtained in violation of the 4th and 5th Amendments to the U.S. Constitution, and was established Weeks v. U.S. and extended to the states in Mapp v.Ohio?

a. The Exclusionary Rule
b. The Good Faith Exception
c. Fruit of the Poisoned Tree
d. The Automobile Exception

5.13   What was the Star Chamber?

a. A secret room where the King of England conferred with his advisors.
b. An English court interrogation room where confessions were forced via the use of torture.
c. A room in Buckingham Palace decorated with paintings of constellations on the ceiling.
d. None of the above.

5.14   What Amendment protects us against self incrimination?

a. 1st Amendment
b. 4th Amendment
c. 5th Amendment
d. 7th Amendment

5.15   In what landmark case did the Court rule that confessions obtained by force were tainted?

a. Olmstead v. United States
b. Ashcraft v. Tennessee
c. Leyra v. Denno
d. Brown v. Mississippi

5.16   What landmark case established the defendant's right to an attorney when accused of a crime?

a. Gideon v. Wainwright
b. Brown v. Mississippi
c. Leyra v. Denno
d. Olmstead v. United States.

5.17   In what year was the Miranda decision handed down by the Supreme Court?

a. 1965
b. 1966
c. 1967
d. 1968

5.18   What president created the National Crime Commission?

a. Hoover
b. Kennedy
c. Coolidge
d. Ford

5.19   Where did the Knapp Commission operate?
        a. Boston
        b. Los Angeles
        c. Chicago
        d. New York

5.20   Which below is an example of an investigative commission?
        a. The Mollen Commission
        b. Internal Affairs
        c. The Police Act of 1976
        d. Citizen Oversight Boards

5.21   What established the Police Complaints Board to handle complaints of police misconduct
        in England?
        a. The Law Enforcement Act of 1977
        b. The British Police Code of 1976
        c. The Police Act of 1976
        d. The Police Complaint Act of 1977

5.22   The most common law suits against the police are based on allegations of:
        a. Wrongful death
        b. Negligent practices
        c. Police brutality
        d. Wrongful arrest

5.23   Most lawsuits against federal law enforcement agents are governed by:
        a. The Federal Employees Liability Reform and Tort Compensation Act
        b. Bivens Actions
        c. The Westfall Act.
        d. Both a and c are correct.

5.24   What case opened up the federal courts for suits against federal government officials for
        denial of constitutional rights?
        a. Bivens v. Six Unknown Federal Agents
        b. Jacobsen v. United States
        c. Escobedo v. Illinois
        d. Federal agents cannot be sued for damages resulting from their actions on the job.

5.25   When can the police use deadly force against a fleeing felon?
        a. When a felony crime has been committed.
        b. If the felon attempts to escape.
        c. When there is clear and present danger to the public.
        d. When a misdemeanor crime has been committed.

CHAPTER SIX

6.1   Laws passed in the southern states after the Civil War to disenfranchise free slaves were
        called:
        a. Black Codes
        b. Jim Crow Laws
        c. Colored Codes
        d. Negro Laws

6.2   The Bow Street Runners were:
        a. Paid law enforcement officers.
        b. A gang of thieves operating out of the Bow Street docks.
        c. A private thief-taking organization.
        d. A British rock band.

6.3   What did the Urban Cohort do?
        a. Protect the emperor and his property.
        b. Maintain public order among citizens.
        c. Wage war against the enemies of Rome.
        d. All of the above.

6.4   What were magistrates called in Rome?
        a. Praetors
        b. Quaestores
        c. Magisrates
        d. Cohortes

6.5   Ten tithings were known as a:
        a. Cohort
        b. Frankpledge
        c. Hundred
        d. Thousand

6.6   The power of the shire-reeve to summon citizens assistance was known as:
        a. The Frankpledge
        b. Lex talionus
        c. Tithing
        d. Posse comitatus

6.7   When did King Henry I issue the Legis Henrici?
        a. 1116
        b. 1216
        c. 1016
        d. 1316

6.8   How many judicial districts did the Legis Henrici divide England into?
        a. 20
        b. 30
        c. 40
        d. 50

6.9   What king signed the Magna Carta?
        a. King Henry XVII
        b. King William I
        c. King Henry II
        d. King John I

6.10   In what year did King George II allow city councils to levy taxes to pay for the night
        watch?
        a. 1737
        b. 1742
        c. 1763
        d. 1786

6.11   Who started the Bow Street Runners?
        a. Robert Peel
        b. Henry Fielding
        c. George Gordon
        d. John Fielding

6.12   What were Peel's professional police officers called?
        a. Robbies
        b. P.C. Plods
        c. Bobbies
        d. Blue Hats

6.13   When did Philadelphia crate a night watch and a day watch police force?
        a. 1830
        b. 1840
        c. 1850
        d. 1860

6.14   What Article of the Constitution states that any power not enumerated in the Constitution
        as a federal government power is a state government power?
        a. V
        b. III
        c. VII
        d. X

6.15   In what year did the Civil War begin?
        a. 1860
        b. 1861
        c. 1862
        d. 1863

6.16   The system of policing which used kinship associations common in the Middle Ages in
        England was known as:
        a. The Frankpledge
        b. The feudal system
        c. The watch and ward
        d. The Common Law

6.17   The first black police officer was appointed where?
        a. New York City
        b. Selma, AL
        c. Houston, TX
        d. Jackson, MS

6.18   Laws aimed specifically at nullifying the rights granted to recently freed slaves were
        called:
        a. Slave codes
        b. Black laws
        c. Black codes
        d. Freeman laws

6.19   What landmark case established the doctrine of "separate but equal?"
        a. Plessy v. Ferguson
        b. Plessy v. U.S.
        c. Ferguson v. Plessy
        d. Ferguson v. U.S.

6.20   Where was August Vollmer Chief of Police?
        a. New York City
        b. Boston
        c. Houston
        d. Berkeley

6.21   When was the Posse Comitatus Act passed?
        a. 1877
        b. 1878
        c. 1879
        d. 1880

6.22   What act established the U.S. Marshal Service?
        a. The Judiciary Act of 1789
        b. The Marshall's Act of 1790
        c. The Crime Control Act of 1859
        d. The Posse Comitatus Act of 1878

6.23   The earliest known example of legal codes defining crimes and civil offenses was:
        a. The Code of Hammurabi
        b. The Bible
        c. The Twelve Roman Tablets
        d. The Magna Carta

6.24   What federal agency runs the Missile Escort Program?
        a. The U.S. Secret Service
        b. The Bureau of Alcohol, Tobacco, and Firearms
        c. The U.S. Marshall's Service
        d. The Federal Bureau of Investigation

6.25   Who was not a deputy U.S. Marshal?
        a. Wild Bill Hickok
        b. Buffalo Bill Cody
        c. Kit Carson
        d. Bat Masterson

CHAPTER SEVEN

7.1   Where do many people get most of their information about the police?
a. College textbooks
b. Scholarly journal articles
c. Personal experience
d. The media

7.2   How many police agencies are there in America?
a. 17,000
b. 15,000
c. 12,000
d. 10,000

7.3   The title of the second in command of a municipal police agency is:
a. Major
b. Deputy Chief
c. Captain
d. Chief Deputy

7.4   How many federal law enforcement agencies are well known to the public?
a. Ten
b. One hundred
c. Six
d. Two

ANSWER: c

7.5   The geographical jurisdiction of a municipal police officer:
a. Ends at the city limits.
b. Extends into the surrounding county.
c. Extends throughout the state.
d. Ends at the geographical boundaries of his beat.

7.6   How long are the elected terms of most modern sheriff's?
a. Two years
b. Three years
c. Four years
d. Five years

7.7   The oldest local policing authority in the U.S. is the:
        a. Constable
        b. Sheriff
        c. Chief
        d. Shire-reeve

7.8   The geographical jurisdiction of the sheriff is the:
        a. County
        b. City
        c. State
        d. Territory

7.9   What percentage of sheriff's departments employ fewer than ten full time deputies?
        a. 50%
        b. 25%
        c. 71%
        d. 43%

7.10   What percentage of municipal police agencies employ less than 50 officers?
        a. 70%
        b. 90%
        c. 50%
        d. 30%

7.11   What division is typically the largest organizational unit in a police agency?
        a. Patrol
        b. Support
        c. Detectives
        d. Drugs

7.12   How many years are patrol officers commonly expected to serve before they become
        eligible to become a detective?
        a. 5 to 10
        b. 1 to 5
        c. 3 to 6
        d. 10 to 12

7.13   The chief executive officer of a state's highway patrol is normally called a:
        a. Chief
        b. Commander
        c. Director
        d. Supervisor

7.14   The jurisdiction of a state police agency:
       a. Is limited to the interstate highways.
       b. Does not include crime control functions.
       c. Is restricted within city limits.
       d. Extends throughout the geographical boundaries of the state.

7.15   How do police chiefs get their jobs?
       a. They are appointed.
       b. They are elected.
       c. They are drafted.
       d. None of the above.

7.16   The only elected position in law enforcement is the:
       a. Police Commissioner
       b. Sheriff
       c. Chief of Police
       d. Police Superintendent

7.17   Most federal law enforcement agencies have jurisdiction in:
       a. All 50 states
       b. The District of Columbia
       c. U.S. territories
       d. All of the above.

7.18   How many national police agencies does France have?
       a. 4
       b. 1
       c. 2
       d. None

7.19   Who handles law enforcement on Indian reservations?
       a. Tribal police
       b. County Sheriff
       c. Municipal police
       d. FBI

7.20   When was the Office of Tribal Justice formed?
       a. 1921
       b. 1890
       c. 1995
       d. That office does not exist.

7.21   The largest employer of federal officers is the:
      a. Bureau of Prisons
      b. Immigration and Naturalization Service
      c. Bureau of Alcohol, Tobacco and Firearms
      d. The Federal Bureau of Investigation

7.22   The DEA was founded in the year:
      a. 1973
      b. 1965
      c. 1921
      d. 1945

7.23   Who operates the National Police Academy?
      a. DEA
      b. CIA
      c. FBI
      d. International Association of Chiefs of Police

7.24   What did the Lindbergh Law do?
      a. Made kidnapping a capitol offense.
      b. Made kidnapping a felony.
      c. Made kidnapping a crime.
      d. A and C are correct.

7.25   What president created the Bureau of Investigation?
      a. Kennedy
      b. Lincoln
      c. Hoover
      d. Roosevelt

CHAPTER EIGHT

8.1   Minorities and women were effectively banned from police work until the Civil Rights
        Act of 1964 was amended in:
        a. 1972
        b. 1965
        c. 1978
        d. 1980

8.2   What rules mandate that positions in law enforcement be filled by competitive evaluation
        of the candidates based on job related criteria?
        a. State statute
        b. Civil service rules
        c. Constitutional mandate
        d. None of the above.

8.3   Which below isn't part of the usual hiring process for a new law enforcement officer?
        a. Written exam
        b. Oral interview
        c. Psychological testing
        d. All of the above are part of the hiring process.

8.4   One of the biggest differences between employment in a federal agency and a local or
        state agency is:
        a. Pay
        b. Benefits
        c. Jurisdiction
        d. Organizational structure

8.5   Police and sheriff's departments employ about how many full-time, sworn officers?
        a. 500,000
        b. 1 million
        c. 1.5 million
        d. 250,000

8.6   The voluntary rating of police departments according to standards set by CALEA, and
        designed to promote police professionalism is known as:
        a. Qualification
        b. Professionalization
        c. Underwriting
        d. Accreditation

8.7   Where is the FBI Training Center located?
        a. Quantico, VA
        b. Los Angeles, CA
        c. Miami, FL
        d. Glenyco, GA

8.8   At what age can you legally own a pistol?
        a. 21
        b. 18
        c. 16
        d. 25

8.9   Most law enforcement agencies require that applicants be a minimum of what age?
        a. 25
        b. 20
        c. 21
        d. 22

8.10   The style of policing that emphasizes physical expression and interaction between police
        and the public that reflects the values of lower middle class and urban communities is
        referred to as:
        a. Watchman
        b. Blue collar
        c. Legalistic
        d. Community oriented

8.11   What percentage of larger police agencies use laptop computers?
        a. 25%
        b. 12%
        c. 30%
        d. 15%

8.12   The purpose of the written examination in the police hiring process is:
        a. To test the applicant's knowledge of the law.
        b. To evaluate the applicant's handwriting.
        c. To test for basic skills that will not be part of the academy curriculum.
        d. None of the above.

8.13   What questions generally cannot be asked of the police applicant?
        a. Their religious orientation.
        b. Their educational background.
        c. Their ethnic origin.
        d. A and C are correct.

8.14   Which infraction will disqualify an applicant from police service?
       a. An arrest for drunk driving.
       b. An arrest for violence.
       c. An arrest for drug violations.
       d. All the above will disqualify an applicant from police service.

8.15   What percentage of police departments require a psychological evaluation as part of the hiring process?
       a. 80%
       b. 70%
       c. 60%
       d. 50%

8.16   What percentage of agencies reserve the right to polygraph an applicant?
       a. 75%
       b. 55%
       c. 45%
       d. 35%

8.17   How many questions does the MMPI contain?
       a. 250
       b. 500
       c. 600
       d. 725

8.18   Which of the disorders listed below does the MMPI not provide a score on?
       a. Depression
       b. Psychosis
       c. Paranoia
       d. Hypochondriasis

8.19   How many hours of training do most police officers receive in police academy?
       a. 400-1,100
       b. 1,000- 1,200
       c. 600-800
       d. 250-500

8.20   How long is the average police academy?
       a. 1,000 hours
       b. 600 hours
       c. 450 hours
       d. 800 hours

8.21 POST stands for:
a. Police Officer Standard Tracking Commission
b. Police Organizational Standards and Training Commission
c. Police Officer Standards and Training Commission
d. Police Officer Standardized Training Continuum

8.22 Most new police officers are kept on probationary status for:
a. Up to one year.
b. Up to six months.
c. Only a few weeks.
d. About eight weeks.

8.23 What style of policing is usually adopted by cities with homogenous populations with strong traditional mayor-controlled police departments?
a. Service style
b. Watchman style
c. Legalistic style
d. A and C are correct.

8.24 What style of policing emphasizes the role of the police officer as crime fighter and rule enforcer?
a. Service style
b. Watchman style
c. Legalistic Style
d. White-collar policing

8.25 The belief that ignoring public order violations and disruptive behavior leads to community neglect, which fosters further disorder and crime is called:
a. The community empowerment theory.
b. Community policing.
c. Problem oriented policing.
d. The broken window theory.

CHAPTER NINE

9.1   Who did Aaron Burr kill in a duel in the year 1804?
       a. John Adams
       b. Thomas Jefferson
       c. Alexander Hamilton
       d. Ben Franklin

9.2   Where was Hammurabi king?
       a. Greece
       b. Babylon
       c. Egypt
       d. Rome

9.3   What legal code forms the basis of the American system of jurisprudence?
       a. English Common Law
       b. The Code of Hammurabi
       c. The Justinian Code
       d. The Napoleonic Code

9.4   Which Amendment to the Constitution restricted the jurisdiction of the federal courts by
       declaring that a private citizen from one state cannot sue the government of another state
       in federal court?
       a. 12th
       b. 10th
       c. 11th
       d. 9th

9.5   Where is the jurisdiction of the federal courts defined in the Constitution?
       a. Article 1, Section 4
       b. Article 4, Section 3
       c. Article 2, Section 1
       d. Article 3, Section 2

9.6   A private wrong that causes physical harm to another is called:
       a.   A crime
       b.   A Tort
       c.   Liability
       d.   Civil law

9.7   The standard of proof in a civil trial is:
       a. A preponderance of the evidence.
       b. Beyond a reasonable doubt.
       c. Beyond any doubt.
       d. None of the above.

9.8   The landmark case that established the power and role of the Supreme Court was:
       a. Miranda v. Arizona
       b. In re Gault
       c. Mapp v. Ohio
       d. Marbury v. Madison

9.9   How many courts make up the federal judiciary?
       a. 13
       b. 50
       c. 100
       d. 75

9.10   How many federal judicial circuits are there?
       a. 13
       b. 12
       c. 11
       d. 10

9.11   What created the Federal Magistrate courts?
       a. Constitutional mandate
       b. The Federal Magistrate's Act of 1968
       c. The Supreme Court
       d. Presidential Decree

9.12   A concise statement of the main points of a law case is called a:
       a. Warrant
       b. Writ
       c. Review
       d. Brief

9.13   How many United States Circuit Courts of Appeal are there?
       a. 13
       b. 40
       c. 25
       d. 80

9.14   What Amendment to the Constitution initiated Prohibition?
        a. 15th
        b. 18th
        c. 12th
        d. 20th

ANSWER: b

9.15   What Amendment to the Constitution ended Prohibition?
        a. 18th
        b. 19th
        c. 21st
        d. 20th

9.16   The "court of last resort" is the:
        a. U.S. District Court
        b. U.S. Circuit Court
        c. U.S. Magistrate's Court
        d. U.S. Supreme Court

9.17   In 1999, what percentage of cases that it reviewed did the Supreme Court reverse?
        a. 25%
        b. 50%
        c. 15%
        d. 30%

9.18   What established the Pennsylvania Supreme Court?
        a. The Pennsylvania Constitution
        b. The Judiciary Act of 1722
        c. The Constitution of 1968
        d. All the above.

9.19   The intermediate appellate courts in the state court system are called:
        a. Circuit courts
        b. Courts of last resort
        c. District courts
        d. Appellate Courts

9.20   Who was Myra Bradwell?
        a. The first female Supreme Court justice
        b. The first woman admitted to the Illinois bar.
        c. A law professor at Harvard.
        d. None of the above.

9.21   The standardized test that measures a prospective law student's analytical thinking and
       writing abilities is called the:
       a. LSAT
       b. SATS
       c. MMPI
       d. None of the above.

9.22   How many years does a junior barrister have to practice before he can apply for
       promotion to Queen's Counsel?
       a. 1 to 5
       b. 5 to 10
       c. 10 to 15
       d. 15 to 20

9.23   How are federal judges removed from office?
       a. They are fired.
       b. They are disbarred.
       c. They are impeached.
       d. They are demoted.

9.24   What two states don't require that trial court judges have a law degree?
       a. Alabama and Mississippi
       b. Maine and Massachusetts
       c. Texas and Idaho
       d. Tennessee and Kansas

9.25   How does the U.S. Supreme Court notify a lower court that it intends to review the record
       of a case?
       a. The Court issues a writ of certiorari.
       b. The Court issues a brief.
       c. The Court issues a writ of habeas corpus.
       d. The Court issues a notice of intention to review.

CHAPTER TEN

10.1   Which is not a court of limited jurisdiction?
    a. Municipal courts
    b. State court
    c. Justice of the peace courts
    d. County court

10.2   Where do most felony criminal trials take place?
    a. State courts of general jurisdiction
    b. The U.S. Supreme Court
    c. United States District Courts
    d. A and C are correct.

10.3   Which Amendment to the Constitution prohibits double jeopardy?
    a. 5th
    b. 4th
    c. 2nd
    d. 1st

10.4   The ultimate power of the prosecutor to decide if a criminal case will go to trial is called:
    a. Prosecutorial authority
    b. Prosecutorial discretion
    c. Prosecutorial power
    d. Prosecutorial decision-making

10.5   When did the Norman Conquest of England occur?
    a. 1044
    b. 1055
    c. 1066
    d. 1077

10.6   Money or property pledged to insure a defendant shows up for a trial is called:
    a. Frankpledge
    b. Bail
    c. Weregild
    d. Manprice

10.7   Which Amendment to the Constitution addresses the issue of bail?
    a. 3rd
    b. 5th
    c. 7th
    d. 8th

10.8   When did state judiciaries begin to enact danger laws that allowed courts to deny bail for certain offenses where public safety was a concern?
a. 1970s
b. 1950s
c. 1980s
d. 1960s

10.9   What legislation authorized federal judges to deny bail to alleged offenders when public safety was a concern?
a. The 1980 Dangerous Crimes Act
b. The 1984 Bail Reform Act
c. The1992 Criminal Predator's Act
d. None of the above.

10.10   What percentage of the bail do bail bondspersons generally charge as a fee?
a. 25%
b. 15%
c. 10%
d. 20%

10.11   When did the Manhattan Bail Project take place?
a. 1950s
b. 1970s
c. 1980s
d. 1960s

10.12   What provides for the pretrial release of the accused based on his unsecured promise to return for trial?
a. Release on recognizance
b. Unsecured bond
c. Property bond
d. Bail

10.13   What allows the court to release a pretrial defendant to the custody of an individual or agency that promises to be responsible for their behavior and to guarantee their participation in the legal process?
a. Conditional release
b. Signature bond
c. Third-party custody
d. All of the above.

10.14   How are most criminal cases disposed of?
a. Trial
b. Plea bargaining
c. Dismissal
d. Guilty pleas

10.15   The court's docket is also known as its:
        a. Calendar
        b. Record
        c. Address
        d. Organization

10.16   Which Amendment to the Constitution guarantees the right to a speedy trial?
        a. 1st
        b. 4th
        c. 5th
        d. 6th

10.17   In what case did the Supreme Court rule that a defendant's failure to demand a speedy trial does not amount to a waiver of the 6th Amendment right?
        a. Klopfer v. North Carolina
        b. Barker v. Wingo
        c. Wingo v. North Carolina
        d. Barker v. Klopfer

10.18   When was the Speedy Trial Act passed?
        a. 1974
        b. 1964
        c. 1954
        d. 1944

10.19   The Speedy Trial Act requires that a federal case be brought to trial within how many days after the suspect is arrested?
        a. 30
        b. 70
        c. 100
        d. 125

10.20   A motion filed by the defense requesting that the prosecution turn over all relevant evidence and a list of witnesses to be used by the prosecution at the trial is called:
        a. Motion for continuance
        b. Motion for change of venue
        c. Motion for discovery
        d. Motion for suppression

10.21   What motion allows the defense to receive details as to exactly what items found in a defendant's possession are considered illegal by the prosecution?
        a. Motion for a Bill of Particulars
        b. Motion for Suppression
        c. Motion for Discovery
        d. Motion for Continuance

10.22   Who isn't part of the courtroom work group?
   a. Judge
   b. Bailiff
   c. Defense attorney
   d. All the above are members of the court room work group.

10.23   The calendar on which court cases are scheduled for trial is called the:
   a. Court calendar
   b. Court docket
   c. Court schedule
   d. Court list

10.24   Who below is not a part of the courtroom workgroup?
   a. The victim
   b. The judge
   c. The bailiff
   d. The clerk of court

10.25   When an attorney handles a case for free, it is called:
   a. Fee simple
   b. Trial de novo
   c. Pro bono
   d. Public defense

CHAPTER ELEVEN

11.1   Which of the below isn't a form of corporal punishment?
a. Whipping
b. Economic servitude
c. Dunking
d. Pillory

11.2   When an individual who has committed a crime is deterred from committing future crimes we call it:
a. Specific deterrence
b. Individual deterrence
c. General deterrence
d. Organized deterrence

11.3   The ability to prevent non-offenders from committing crimes is called:
a. Specific deterrence
b. Individual deterrence
c. General deterrence
d. Organized deterrence

11.4   A two part trial structure in which the jury first determines guilt or innocence and then determines the appropriate punishment is called:
a. A two phase trial
b. A capitol trial
c. A trial de novo
d. A bifurcated trial

11.5   Who first popularized the idea that a tendency toward criminal behavior was inherited?
a. Cesare Beccara
b. Edwin Sutherland
c. Cesar Lombroso
d. Sheldon Gulick

11.6   What state uses banishment as a punishment for crime?
a. Georgia
b. Tennessee
c. Kentucky
d. A and C are both correct.

11.7   What correctional philosophy calls for the treatment and cure of the offender?
        a. Rehabilitation
        b. Retribution
        c. Incapacitation
        d. Restorative Justice

11.8   Which correctional model advocates the needs of the victim?
        a. Retribution
        b. Restorative Justice
        c. Incapacitation
        d. Rehabilitation

11.9   Who determines guilt in a bench trial?
        a. The jury
        b. The prosecutor
        c. The judge
        d. The defense counsel

11.10   Who is responsible for determining what a convicted offenders sentence will be?
        a. The state legislature
        b. The prosecutor
        c. The judge
        d. The jury

11.11   What Amendment to the Constitution addresses the sentencing of convicted offenders?
        a. 8th
        b. 5th
        c. 10th
        d. 2nd

11.12   Which president signed an executive order subjecting terrorist defendants to trial by
        military tribunal?
        a. Carter
        b. Bush
        c. Clinton
        d. Reagan

11.13   Punishment for a misdemeanor cannot exceed:
        a. Five years in prison.
        b. A fine of 1,000.
        c. One year in prison.
        d. Eighteen months in prison.

11.14   The sentencing model in which the offender is sentenced to a fixed term of incarceration
        is called:
        a. Truth in sentencing
        b. Restorative justice
        c. Intermediate sanctions
        d. Determinate sentencing

11.15   What is used to gather information about a convicted offender to assist the judge in
        determining the best sentence?
        a. Criminal investigation
        b. Post conviction examination
        c. Presentence investigation
        d. None of the above.

11.16   Who conducts federal presentence investigations?
        a. Federal Probation and Parole officers
        b. U.S. Marshals
        c. Investigators assigned to the federal prosecutor's office.
        d. FBI agents

11.17   When was the Insanity Defense Reform Act passed?
        a. 1967
        b. 1984
        c. 1992
        d. 2000

11.18   What determines if an individual should be released or confined to a mental institution?
        a. The federal commitment process
        b. The criminal commitment process
        c. The state commitment process
        d. The civil commitment process

11.19   In what type of case are you most likely to see an insanity defense used?
        a. Homicide
        b. Theft
        c. Assault and battery
        d. Arson

11.20   *Mens rea* means:
        a. Guilty act
        b. Sick mind
        c. Guilty mind
        d. Criminal act

11.21   Which below isn't a structured sentencing model?
  a. Determinate sentencing
  b. Indeterminate sentencing
  c. Mandatory sentencing
  d. Presumptive sentencing

11.22   "Three strikes" laws are an example of:
  a. Presumptive sentencing
  b. Mandatory sentencing
  c. Determinate sentencing
  d. Indeterminate sentencing

11.23   If you are convicted of a Class E felony, what is the maximum sentence you can receive?
  a. Death
  b. 25 years
  c. 10 years
  d. 5 years

11.24   If you are convicted of a Class B misdemeanor, what is the minimum sentence you will receive?
  a. 30 days
  b. 1 year
  c. 60 days
  d. Probation

11.25   What document does a judge use to assist in determining an appropriate sentence?
  a. Federal Conviction Guideline Manual
  b. Federal Trial Guideline Manual
  c. Federal Sentencing Guideline Manual
  d. None of the above.

CHAPTER TWELVE

12.1   Who was the first warden of the Main State Prison?
a. John Claton
b. Daniel Rose
c. Edward Fuller
d. James Owens

12.2   In the 1600s, the most common punishment for crime was:
a. Corporal punishment
b. Capitol punishment
c. Fines
d. A and B are both correct.

12.3   In England, branding as a form of punishment dates to:
a. The first century, AD
b. The second century, AD
c. The fourth century, AD
d. The third century, AD

12.4   Prisons for inmates considered to be at high risk of escape or who are dangerously violent to other inmates or staff are called:
a. Maximum security prisons
b. Medium security prisons
c. Supermax prisons
d. Country club prisons

12.5   The most common forms of mutilation used in colonial America were:
a. Cutting off the hands and feet.
b. Cutting off the nose
c. Scarring the cheeks
d. Cutting off the ears and tongues.

12.6   What law established whipping as a punishment for vagrants in 16th century England?
a. The Punishment Act of 1520
b. The Whipping Act of 1530
c. The Statute of Westminster
d. The Magna Carta

12.7   In what year did the last known dunking take place in England?
a. 1820
b. 1845
c. 1830
d. 1810

12.8   When did the U.S. Congress abolish whipping as a punishment in America?
        a. 1810
        b. 1778
        c. 1790
        d. 1950

12.9   When did Delaware repeal its whipping law?
        a. 1843
        b. 1954
        c. 1981
        d. 1972

12.10   The Bridewell was a:
        a. Poor house
        b. Prison
        c. School
        d. Hospital

12.11   What king ordered jails to be constructed in every shire in the year 1166?
        a. James I
        b. Henry II
        c. William I
        d. Henry I

12.12   When was the Hulks Act passed?
        a. 1700
        b. 1738
        c. 1776
        d. 1792

12.13   France's seaport stockades were turned into permanent prisons called:
        a. Hulks
        b. Gaols
        c. Bagnes
        d. None of the above.

12.14   Who wrote *State of the Prisons*?
        a. Ben Franklin
        b. John Howard
        c. Daniel Webster
        d. James Addams

12.15 Where was the Walnut Street Jail located?
   a. Philadelphia
   b. New York
   c. Boston
   d. Chicago

12.16 Where was Eastern State Penitentiary built?
   a. New York
   b. Pennsylvania
   c. Maryland
   d. Vermont

12.17 What system required that prisoners communicate only with guards or prison officials?
   a. The obedience system
   b. The quiet system
   c. The orderly system
   d. The silent system

12.18 Cutting off body parts as punishment for criminal offenses is called:
   a. Capitol punishment
   b. Just deserts
   c. Mutilation
   d. Corporal punishment

12.19 The southern system that used inmate labor to maintain large profit making prison farms
   is called the:
   a. Prison farm system
   b. Prison industry system
   c. Convict agricultural system
   d. Convict lease system

12.20 In order to supply labor once provided by slaves, southern prisons practiced:
   a. The indentured servant system.
   b. The convict lease system.
   c. The forced labor system.
   d. Chain gangs

12.21 How many years after opening did it take for Auburn Prison to become financially
   independent?
   a. 20
   b. 15
   c. 35
   d. 13

12.22 Chain gangs originated in:
       a. Southern prisons
       b. Northern prisons
       c. England
       d. France

12.23 The trend toward the use of for profit jails and prisons run by private companies is
       called?
       a. Prisons for profit
       b. Privatization
       c. The convict lease system
       d. Prison industries

12.24 How many inmates died in the Attica prison riot of 1971?
       a. 12
       b. 20
       c. 43
       d. 65

12.25 What percentage of female inmates in state prisons report that they were sexually or
       physically abused before they went to prison?
       a. 57%
       b. 47%
       c. 87%
       d. 27%

CHAPTER THIRTEEN

13.1   About how many people were on probation in the United States at the end of the year 2000?
a. 3.7 million
b. 5.1 million
c. 4.6 million
d. 2.9 million

13.2   Since the 1970s, the number of individuals incarcerated in state prisons has increased by what percentage?
a. 500%
b. 200%
c. 600%
d. 300%

13.3   What state closed five small, privately operated, minimum security prisons in 2002?
a. Tennessee
b. California
c. Georgia
d. North Carolina

13.4   What criminal justice option offers the defendant an alternative to a trial, conviction and sentencing?
a. Parole
b. Suspended sentence
c. Probation
d. Diversion

13.5   What sentencing option diverts the offender after conviction but prior to his serving prison time?
a. Boot camp
b. Parole
c. Probation
d. Suspension

13.6   When does mandatory release occur?
a. When the inmate has served two-thirds of his sentence.
b. When the inmate has served the entire length of their maximum sentence.
c. When the inmate is approved for parole.
d. When the inmate is given a suspended sentence.

13.7   Good time credits entitle an inmate to:
       a. Early release.
       b. A parole hearing.
       c. Probation.
       d. Additional recreation time.

13.8   An act by a governor or the President that forgives the prisoner and rescinds the sentence
       is called:
       a. Clemency
       b. Commutation of sentence
       c. Forgiveness
       d. Pardon

13.9   What branch of government grants pardons?
       a. Legislative
       b. Judicial
       c. Executive
       d. None of the above.

13.10 Who pardoned Richard Nixon?
       a. Jimmy Carter
       b. George Bush
       c. Ronald Reagan
       d. Gerald Ford

13.11 America's first probation officer was:
       a. John Augustus
       b. Thomas Jefferson
       c. O.W. Wilson
       d. None of the above.

13.12 The sentencing model under which the defendant is sentenced to a prison term with a
       minimum and a maximum number of years to serve is called:
       a. Structured sentencing
       b. Indeterminate sentencing
       c. Determinate sentencing
       d. Mandatory sentencing

13.13 When a defendant is offered an alternative to criminal trial and a prison sentence it is
       called:
       a. Parole
       b. Plea bargaining
       c. Diversion
       d. Probation

13.14 What state passed the first probation statute?
    a. Massachusetts
    b. New York
    c. Maine
    d. Vermont

13.15 How many states had adopted probation by 1920?
    a. 40
    b. 16
    c. 26
    d. 33

13.16 Women make up what percentage of America's probationers?
    a. 12%
    b. 2%
    c. 15%
    d. 22%

13.17 What percentage of adults on probation are white?
    a. 64%
    b. 22%
    c. 34%
    d. 78%

13.18 Who is credited with developing the mark system?
    a. John Augustus
    b. Alexander Maconochie
    c. Douglas Fisk
    d. Ben Franklin

13.19 Who developed the Irish system?
    a. John Augustus
    b. Alexander Maconochie
    c. Walter Crofton
    d. None of the above.

13.20 The first "good time" laws were passed in 1817 in what state?
    a. Maine
    b. New York
    c. Texas
    d. Alabama

13.21   Who determines if an inmate is to receive early release from prison?
a. The parole board
b. The judge
c. The governor
d. The prosecutor

13.22   An early form of parole invented by Sir Walter Crofton under which prisoners were released conditionally on good behavior and were supervised in the community.
a. The Mark system
b. The Diversion system
c. The Irish system
d. The Crofton system

ANSWER: c

13.23   If a state places decision making about parole under the authority of an autonomous parole board, it is using what model?
a. Executive model
b. Autonomous model
c. Federal model
d. Independent model

13.24   If the organization of decision making about parole is a functions of a state's department of corrections, that state is using what model?
a. Consolidated model
b. Federal model
c. Independent model
d. Autonomous model

13.25   What landmark case gave parolees some protection against arbitrary and capricious revocation of parole?
a. Montana v. State
b. Morrissey v. Brewer
c. Cain v. Texas
d. Adams v. U.S.

CHAPTER FOURTEEN

14.1   About how many inmates die in prison each year?
a. 2,500
b. 4,220
c. 3,300
d. 1,850

14.2   Prevention and treatment programs designed to promote the successful transition of the offender from prison to the community are called:
a. Community oriented corrections
b. Diversion programs
c. Alternative corrections
d. Community based corrections

14.3   Most offenders sentenced to prison return to the community within:
a. two years.
b. five years.
c. six months.
d. one year.

14.4   Social work case workers who specialize in helping offenders adjust to life in prison, release from prison, and successful reentry into the community are called:
a. Parole supervisors
b. Parole case managers
c. Correctional case managers
d. Correctional social workers

14.5   What term is used to describe the movement of offenders back and forth between the prison and the community?
a. Maxing out
b. Revolving door
c. Recidivism
d. Early release

14.6   Two-thirds of all parolees are re-arrested within how many years?
a. 2 years
b. 4 years
c. 5 years
d. 3 years

14.7   What does "NIMBY" mean?
a. Not in my back yard.
b. Never in my back yard.
c. Not in my block, you.
d. New inmate monitoring by youth.

14.8   Which below isn't a type of community based corrections?
a. Boot camps
b. House arrest
c. Furloughs
d. All are examples of community corrections.

14.9   Under what type of community based corrections program are inmates placed on
unsupervised release from prison for particular purposes for a certain period of time?
a. Parole
b. Furlough
c. Work release
d. House arrest

14.10   Punishments that restrict offenders' freedom without imprisoning them are called what?
a. Intermediate sanctions
b. Primary sanctions
c. Shock sanctions
d. Community sanctions

14.11   Where is the Vera Institute located?
a. Atlanta
b. Washington D. C.
c. New York
d. New Orleans

14.12   Which below is not a role of the probation/parole officer?
a. Law enforcement officer
b. Counselor
c. Caseworker
d. Community resource broker

14.13   How many states have intensive probation supervision programs?
a. 40
b. 32
c. 50
d. 15

14.14   Transition programs that allow inmates to move from prison to the community via the use of residential centers are called:
a. Half way houses
b. Intensive probation supervision
c. Furlough
d. Work release

14.15   A national, federally supported crime prevention program that helps states reduce their crime rates by weeding out offenders and restoring neighborhoods.
a. Weed and seed
b. Problem oriented policing
c. Community policing
d. Saturation patrol

14.16   Who is a likely candidate for a boot camp?
a. A mature, violent felon.
b. A mature, non-violent offender.
c. A young violent offender.
d. A young, non-violent offender

14.17   The first shock incarceration law was passed in:
a. Ohio
b. Georgia
c. Washington
d. California

14.18   Programs that allow prisons to release inmates to work at jobs in the community during the day and then return to prison at night are called:
a. Furloughs
b. Work release programs
c. Halfway houses
d. None of the above.

14.19   How many juveniles have died while attending private boot camps?
a. 12
b. 20
c. 30
d. 42

14.20   In what state was electronic monitoring initiated?
a. Florida
b. Georgia
c. Texas
d. New Mexico

14.21 What law first initiated work release as a correctional option?
       a. The Prisoner Rehabilitation Act of 1965
       b. The Reentry partnership Initiative
       c. U.S. Code Title 18, Section 3624
       d. The Huber Law

14.22 A sentence imposed on a first time, non-violent offender who was not expecting a
       sentence, intended to impress upon the offender he possible consequences of their
       behavior by exposing them to a brief period of imprisonment prior to probation.
       a. Shock probation
       b. Shock incarceration
       c. Shock parole
       d. Shock sentencing

14.23 What is the estimated minimum cost per year to house a convicted offender in prison?
       a. $35,000
       b. $22,000
       c. $36,000
       d. $27,000

14.24 When were the first halfway houses opened in the U.S.?
       a. 1760
       b. 1920
       c. 1850
       d. 1950

14.25 The bureau of Justice Statistics estimates that what percentage of federal and state
       inmates and probationers could be characterized as drug involved?
       a. One half
       b. Three fourths
       c. Two thirds
       d. One third

CHAPTER FIFTEEN

15.1   By what percentage did workplace violence decline between 1993 and 1999?
         a. 28%
         b. 13%
         c. 39%
         d. 44%

15.2   *Mens rea* means:
         a. Guilty mind.
         b. Evil behavior.
         c. Guilty act.
         d. Mentally ill.

15.3   That area of criminal justice aimed at fighting cybercrime is known as:
         a. Internet security
         b. Computer security
         c. Web security
         d. Cyber security

15.4   Most juvenile murderers are:
         a. Female
         b. Mentally ill.
         c. Under age 15.
         d. Male.

15.5   Most of the victims of juvenile homicide are killed with a:
         a. Gun.
         b. Knife.
         c. Vehicle.
         d. Poison.

15.6   What percentage of victims of juvenile homicide were strangers to the killer?
         a. 14%
         b. 55%
         c. 31%
         d. 27%

15.7   Crimes committed by corporate executives are called:
        a. Corporate crimes
        b. Torts
        c. White collar crime
        d. Organized crime

15.8   What film did Michael Carneal tell investigators influenced him to commit homicide?
        a. *Die Hard*
        b. *The Basketball Diaries*
        c. *The Good Son*
        d. *Strange World*

15.9   How many acts of violence has the typical child viewed in the media by age 18?
        a. 25,000
        b. 100,000
        c. 250,000
        d. 200,000

15.10   How many people did Charles Whitman kill?
        a. 14
        b. 10
        c. 16
        d. 9

15.11   Blacks make up what percentage of America's imprisoned drug offenders?
        a. 55%
        b. 30%
        c. 62%
        d. 79%

15.12   Blacks make up what percentage of the American population?
        a. 13%
        b. 25%
        c. 10%
        d. 37%

15.13   When was the Harrison Narcotics Act passed?
        a. 1909
        b. 1914
        c. 1920
        d. 1924

15.14 What act made it illegal to use, possess, or sell marijuana?
a. The Harrison Narcotics Act
b. The Marijuana Tax Act
c. The Boggs Act
d. The Omnibus Crime Control Act

15.15 Which act created enhanced penalties for drug use or trafficking in "drug-free school zones?"
a. The Anti-Drug Abuse Act
b. The Harrison Narcotics Act
c. The Comprehensive Drug Abuse Prevention and Control Act
d. The Crime Control Act

15.16 Programs aimed at reducing the demand for drugs by users via the use of educational programs and persuasion are called:
a. Demand reduction programs
b. Decriminalization
c. Supply reduction programs
d. Drug education programs

15.17 Annually how many deaths are attributable to drug abuse?
a. 50,000
b. 66,000
c. 100,000
d. 20,000

15.18 Which below is not a method used by supply reduction programs?
a. Destroy illegal drug crops.
b. Control chemicals needed to manufacture illegal drugs.
c. Educate consumers to the dangers of drug use.
d. Arrest sellers and buyers.

15.19 A program that captures a user's computer and directs it to a web site that the user did into want to go to and cannot exit from except by turning off the computer is called:
a. Page jacking
b. Piggybacking
c. Spamming
d. Denial of service

15.20 The use of the computer to find and steal victims' identities and credentials, usually to make purchases.?
a. Identity theft
b. Piggybacking
c. Spamming
d. Denial of service

15.21   In prison, gangs are known as:
        a. Significant Threat Groups
        b. Security Risk Groups
        c. High Risk Groups
        d. None of the above.

15.22   Most prison gangs are organized:
        a. by religious affiliation.
        b. by race.
        c. by ethnicity.
        d. B and C are correct.

15.23   Which below is not typical prison contraband?
        a. Drugs
        b. Cigarettes
        c. Weapons
        d. All are examples of typical prison contraband.

15.24   Which is not an example of a supply reduction strategy?
        a. Education programs.
        b. Destroy illegal drug crops.
        c. Arrest sellers and buyers.
        d. Control chemicals needed to make illegal drugs.

15.25   What percentage of mentally ill inmates are in prison for a violent crime?
        a. 10%
        b. 25%
        c. 50%
        d. 75%

PRACTICE TEST ANSWER   SHEETS

CHAPTER ONE

1.   c
2.   b
3.   a
4.   c
5.   d
6.   a
7.   c
8.   b
9.   a
10.   a
11.   d
12.   c
13.   c
14.   b
15.   d
16.   a
17.   b
18.   c
19.   a
20.   c
21.   b
22.   b
23.   a
24.   c
25.   d

CHAPTER TWO

1.   c
2.   a
3.   d
4.   b
5.   c
6.   a
7.   c
8.   b
9.   a
10.   b
11.   c
12.   a
13.   d
14.   c

15. c
16. a
17. b
18. a
19. d
20. c
21. a
22. b
23. c
24. a
25 b

CHAPTER THREE

1. a
2. b
3. c
4. d
5. b
6. a
7. d
8. c
9. c
10. a
11. b
12. c
13. d
14. a
15. c
16. b
17. a
18. d
19. b
20. b
21. a
22. b
23. c
24. a
25. b

CHAPTER FOUR

1. c
2. a
3. d
4. c

5.   a
6.   d
7.   b
8.   d
9.   a
10.   c
11.   b
12.   a
13.   b
14.   c
15.   d
16.   b
17.   a
18.   d
19.   c
20.   a
21.   b
22.   c
23.   b
24.   a
25.   c

CHAPTER FIVE

1.   b
2.   a
3.   c
4.   d
5.   a
6.   b
7.   c
8.   a
9.   c
10.   b
11.   c
12.   a
13.   b
14.   c
15.   d
16.   a
17.   b
18.   c
19.   d
20.   a
21.   c
22.   b
23.   d
24.   a
25.   c

CHAPTER SIX

1.   a
2.   c
3.   b
4.   a
5.   c
6.   d
7.   a
8.   b
9.   d
10.   a
11.   b
12.   c
13.   a
14.   d
15.   b
16.   a
17.   b
18.   c
19.   a
20.   d
21.   b
22.   a
23.   a
24.   c
25.   c

CHAPTER SEVEN

1.   d
2.   a
3.   b
4.   c
5.   a
6.   c
7.   b
8.   a
9.   d
10.   b
11.   a
12.   b
13.   c
14.   d
15.   a
16.   b
17.   d
18.   c
19.   a
20.   c
21.   b
22.   a
23.   c
24.   a
25.   d

CHAPTER EIGHT

1.   a
2.   b
3.   d
4.   c
5.   b
6.   d
7.   a
8.   a
9.   c
10.   b
11.   a
12.   c
13.   d
14.   d
15.   a
16.   b
17.   c
18.   b
19.   a
20.   b
21.   c
22.   a
23.   b
24.   c
25.   d

CHAPTER NINE

1. c
2. b
3. a
4. c
5. d
6. b
7. a
8. d
9. c
10. a
11. b
12. d
13. a
14. b
15. c
16. d
17. a
18. b
19. d
20. b
21. a
22. d
23. c
24. b
25. a

CHAPTER TEN

1.   b
2.   d
3.   a
4.   b
5.   c
6.   b
7.   d
8.   a
9.   b
10.   c
11.   d
12.   a
13.   c
14.   b
15.   a
16.   d
17.   b
18.   a
19.   c
20.   c
21.   a
22.   d
23.   b
24.   a
25.   c

CHAPTER ELEVEN

1.   b
2.   a
3.   c
4.   d
5.   c
6.   d
7.   a
8.   b
9.   c
10.   c
11.   a
12.   b
13.   c
14.   d
15.   c
16.   a
17.   b
18.   d
19.   a
20.   c
21.   b
22.   b
23.   d
24.   a
25.   c

CHAPTER TWELVE

1. b
2. d
3. c
4. a
5. d
6. b
7. a
8. c
9. d
10. a
11. b
12. c
13. c
14. b
15. a
16. b
17. d
18. c
19. a
20. b
21. d
22. a
23. b
24. c
25. a

CHAPTER THIRTEEN

1.   c
2.   a
3.   b
4.   d
5.   c
6.   b
7.   a
8.   b
9.   c
10.   d
11.   a
12.   b
13.   c
14.   a
15.   d
16.   d
17.   a
18.   b
19.   c
20.   b
21.   a
22.   c
23.   d
24.   a
25.   b

CHAPTER FOURTEEN

1. c
2. d
3. a
4. c
5. b
6. d
7. a
8. d
9. b
10. a
11. c
12. b
13. c
14. a
15. a
16. d
17. a
18. b
19. c
20. d
21. d
22. a
23. b
24. c
25. c

CHAPTER FIFTEEN

1.   c
2.   a
3.   b
4.   d
5.   a
6.   c
7.   a
8.   b
9.   d
10.   a
11.   c
12.   a
13.   b
14.   c
15.   d
16.   a
17.   d
18.   c
19.   a
20.   a
21.   b
22.   d
23.   d
24.   a
25.   c

Chapter 1

Criminal Justice

© Allyn & Bacon 2005

Introduction

Fear, Terror, and the Criminal Justice System

© Allyn & Bacon 2005

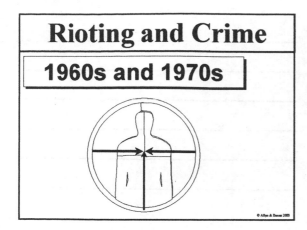

Rioting and Crime

1960s and 1970s

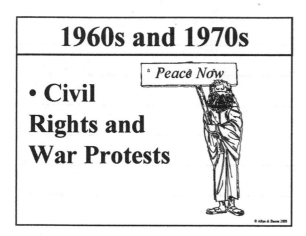

1960s and 1970s

- Civil Rights and War Protests

Peace Now

1960s and 1970s

- The *War on Crime*

CRIMINAL RECORD

JOE LIGHTFINGER

0751200-501064

DEPARTMENT OF CORRECTIONS

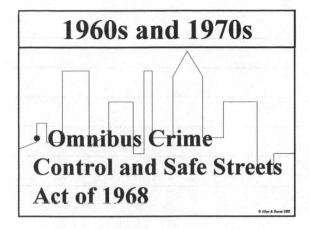

1960s and 1970s

- **Omnibus Crime Control and Safe Streets Act of 1968**

The New Challenge

World Trade Center, Sept. 11, 2001

Safety vs. Freedom

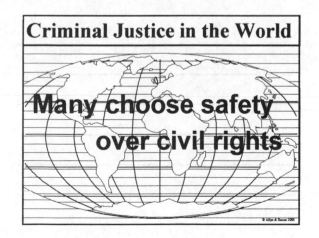

Criminal Justice in the World

Many choose safety over civil rights

Office of Homeland Security

© Allyn & Bacon 2003

Law and Order vs. Individual Rights

Balance between *individual* rights,

    and...

© Allyn & Bacon 2003

Law and Order vs. Individual Rights

...power of the government

© Allyn & Bacon 2003

Law and Order vs. Individual Rights

Civil liberties and Civil Rights

© Allyn & Bacon 2003

Ethics in the System

Foreigners on Death Row

© Allyn & Bacon 2003

Defining Terrorism

- Criminal Justice and Social Justice

- Terrorism and Relativism

© Allyn & Bacon 2003

Defining Terrorism

Diversity in the System:

Freedom Fighters or Terrorists?

War on Terrorism

- **Domestic Terrorism**
- **International Terrorism**
- **Counter terrorism Measures**

Criminal Justice as an Academic Discipline

Study of Criminology and Criminal Justice

Chapter 2

An Overview of the Criminal Justice Process

© Allyn & Bacon 2003

People and Processes in Criminal Justice

The CJ system *detects* and *selects* people to be processed by the system; *processes* them through the system…

© Allyn & Bacon 2003

People and Processes in Criminal Justice

…and provides for a means to *exit* the system

© Allyn & Bacon 2003

Counting Crime

Statistics on crime and research on the three components of the CJ system: police, courts, and corrections…

© Allyn & Bacon 2003

Counting Crime

…drive public policy and changes to address current trends

© Allyn & Bacon 2003

Counting Crime

- Uniform Crime Reports

  Part 1 - 8 crimes
    (Index Crimes)

  Part 2 - 19 crimes

© Allyn & Bacon 2005

Counting Crime

- National Incident - Based Report System

- National Crime Victim Survey

© Allyn & Bacon 2005

Counting Crime

- Campus Crime

- Hate Crimes

- Self-Reports

© Allyn & Bacon 2005

Counting Crime

Crime statistics are a "snapshot of the past"

Indicate what crime has occurred - *not* what crime will occur

© Allyn & Bacon 2005

The Criminal Justice System

- **Agencies and People**

- **Process and Flow**

© Allyn & Bacon 2005

Agencies and People

Police

Courts

Corrections

© Allyn & Bacon 2005

Process and Flow

People accused of a crime *enter* the system; their guilt or innocence is determined,

Process and Flow

and they are punished,

or *exit* the system

Process and Flow

Each agency processes people through their part of the system

No " traffic cop" to direct the flow and process

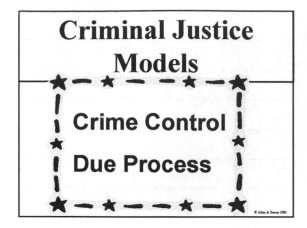

Criminal Justice Models

Crime Control

Due Process

© Allyn & Bacon 2005

State vs. Federal

Criminal Justice Systems

© Allyn & Bacon 2005

International Criminal Justice Systems

© Allyn & Bacon 2005

Criminal Justice in the World
The Globalization of Due Process

© Allyn & Bacon 2005

_____

_____

_____

_____

_____

_____

Chapter 3

This multimedia product and its contents are protected under copyright law. The following are prohibited by law:
• any public performance or display, including transmission of any image over a network;
• preparation of any derivative work, including the extraction, in whole or in part, of any images;
• any rental, lease or lending of the program.

CRIMINAL JUSTICE
JAMES A. FAGIN

Criminal Behavior

Definitions and Causes

© Allyn & Bacon 2003

Moral Perspectives

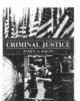

Good vs. Evil

Evolutionary

Theories

© Allyn & Bacon 2003

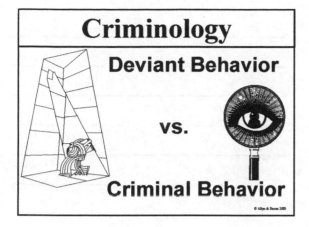

Criminology

Deviant Behavior

vs.

Criminal Behavior

© Allyn & Bacon 2003

Criminology

Roles of theories in Criminology

© Allyn & Bacon 2003

Explanations of Criminal Behavior

© Allyn & Bacon 2003

Explanations of Criminal Behavior

Explanations

- Beccaria and *Classical Theory*

- Bentham and *Neoclassical Theory*

Explanations

- Belief in

Free Will and Individual Choice

Explanations

• The Positive School

Biological Explanations

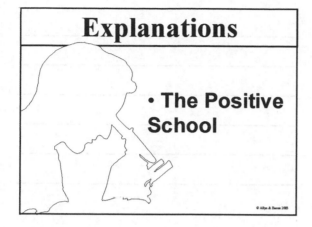

Crime
as an
Inherited Characteristic

Biological Explanations

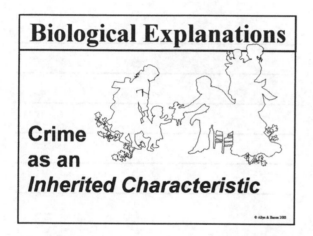

Lombroso
and
Criminality

Biological Explanations

Influence of Biological Determinism

_____

_____

_____

_____

_____

_____

Biological Explanations

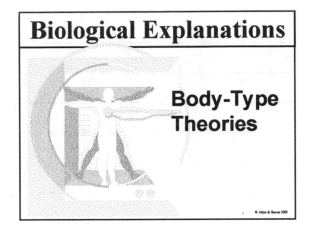

Body-Type Theories

_____

_____

_____

_____

_____

_____

Biological Explanations

Modern Biological Theories

_____

_____

_____

_____

_____

_____

Psychological Explanations

Freud and Psychoanalysis

"Behavior is not a free-will choice, but is controlled by subconscious desires"

© Allyn & Bacon 2003

Psychological Explanations

Personality Theories and Psychopathic Behavior

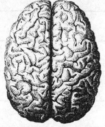

© Allyn & Bacon 2003

Sociological Explanations

• Social Determinism

• Social Disorganization as the Cause of Crime

© Allyn & Bacon 2003

Sociological Explanations

- Social Control Theories
- Strain Theories
- Cultural Deviance Theories
- Conflict Theories

© Allyn & Bacon 2003

Sociological Explanations

Criminal Behavior is *Learned*

© Allyn & Bacon 2003

Chapter 4

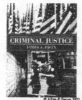

Criminal Law:
Control vs. Liberty

Rule of Law

Standards of behavior are established by rules and procedures that *define* and *prohibit* certain acts as illegal or criminal...

Rule of Law

... and *prescribe punishments* for those acts

© Allyn & Bacon 2003

Making of Law

Federal, state, and local government bodies

© Allyn & Bacon 2003

Making of Law

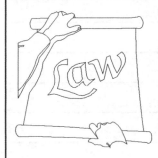

...pass criminal laws to protect citizens

© Allyn & Bacon 2003

Limits of the Law

Criminal law is founded on the principle of rule of law and is based on principles of rationality and justice

© Allyn & Bacon 2003

_____

_____

_____

_____

_____

_____

_____

Limits of the Law

- **Principle of Legality**

- **Ex Post Facto Law**

- **Due Process**

- **Void for Vagueness**

© Allyn & Bacon 2003

_____

_____

_____

_____

_____

_____

Limits of the Law

- **Right to Privacy**

- **Void for Overbreadth**

- **Cruel and Unusual Punishments**

© Allyn & Bacon 2003

_____

_____

_____

_____

_____

_____

_____

Elements of a Crime

The actions and intent of the crime as well as the seriousness of the crime…

© Allyn & Bacon 2003

Elements of a Crime

… all carry weight

in determining punishment

© Allyn & Bacon 2003

Elements of a Crime

Actus reus

• Failure to act (crimes of omission)

• Possession as *actus reus* (possession of prohibited items constitutes *actus reus*)

© Allyn & Bacon 2003

Elements of a Crime

Men's Rea

Intent

- general intent
  - specific intent
    - transferred intent
      - constructive intent

© Allyn & Bacon 2003

Elements of a Crime

Men's Rea

- Strict Liability

- Actions that are criminal without the necessity of any criminal intent

© Allyn & Bacon 2003

Defenses Against Charges

- Alibi

- Consent or condoning by the victim

- Entrapment, frame-up, and outrageous government conduct

© Allyn & Bacon 2003

Defenses Against Charges

- Immunity or Privilege
- Duress, Coercion, Compulsion Drug Condition, and Intoxication
- Mistake or ignorance of Facts of Law

© Allyn & Bacon 2003

Defenses against Charges

- Necessity
- Self-Defense
- Youth
- Insanity

© Allyn & Bacon 2003

Crimes by Law

Model Penal Code classifies crimes into *categories by victims,* as well as defines specific offenses of crimes

© Allyn & Bacon 2003

Crimes by Law

Crimes against Persons

- **Murder**
- **Rape**
- **Robbery**
- **Assault and Battery**

© Allyn & Bacon 2003

Crimes by Law

Crimes against Habitation

- **Burglary**
- **Modern Burglary Statutes**
- **Offenses Related to Burglary**
- **Arson**

© Allyn & Bacon 2003

Crimes by Law

Crimes against Property

- **Larceny**
- **Offenses related to Larceny**

© Allyn & Bacon 2003

Criminal Law

- A pillar of social order

- Constantly changing as society is changing

© Allyn & Bacon 2003

Chapter 5

CRIMINAL JUSTICE
JAMES A. FAGIN

This multimedia product and its contents are protected under copyright law. The following are prohibited by law:

•any public performance or display, including transmission of any image over a network;

•preparation of any derivative work, including the extraction, in whole or in part, of any images;

•any rental, lease or lending of the program.

Copyright © 2003 Allyn and Bacon

Due Process and Police Procedure

Copyright © 2003 Allyn and Bacon

Procedural Law

• Governs the criminal justice system

• Explains how things should be done at each stage of the criminal justice system

Procedural Law

- Includes court procedures (rules of evidence)

- Includes police procedures (search and seizure)

Copyright © 2003 Allyn and Bacon

Rules of Evidence

Police procedure is guided by rules defining what is legal evidence admissible in a court of law

Copyright © 2003 Allyn and Bacon

Exclusionary Rule

- Evidence is *inadmissible* if it is obtained in violation of the U.S. Constitution

- First introduced in 1914, *Weeks v. United States* (applied to federal courts)

Copyright © 2003 Allyn and Bacon

Exclusionary Rule

•1918 - added the *Fruit of the Poisoned Tree* Doctrine:

• If the tree is "poisoned" then the "fruit" of the tree will be also poisoned

Copyright © 2003 Allyn and Bacon

Exclusionary Rule

• 1961 *Mapp v. Ohio* required state courts to use the exclusionary rule

• First case in which evidence gathered illegally was inadmissible in a state court

Copyright © 2003 Allyn and Bacon

Search and Seizure

Rules of evidence define legal search and seizure of places, automobiles, and persons and they define exceptions to the exclusionary rule

Copyright © 2003 Allyn and Bacon

Search and Seizure

Evidence can be obtained by:

- A valid warrant based on probable cause

- Without a warrant while conducting a search incident to lawful arrest

Copyright © 2003 Allyn and Bacon

Search and Seizure

Evidence can be obtained by:

- Plain view searches
- Consent to search
- Search of automobiles

Copyright © 2003 Allyn and Bacon

Ethics in the System

Search of Persons

- Pat-down search- conducted solely to ensure the *safety of the officer*

- Anonymous Tips and Probable Cause

Copyright © 2003 Allyn and Bacon

Search and Seizure

Exceptions to the exclusionary rule:

The Public Safety Exception

- **Fleeing Felon and Deadly Force**

- **The Good Faith Exception**

- **Wire Taps and Privacy**

Copyright © 2003 Allyn and Bacon

Search and Seizure

Interrogations and Confessions

- **Use of physical punishment and pain**
  - **Lying to the suspect**
    - **Police Lineups**
      - **Right to an Attorney**

Copyright © 2003 Allyn and Bacon

Search and Seizure

- **Arrests**

- **Miranda**

- **Entrapment and Police Intelligence Activities**

Copyright © 2003 Allyn and Bacon

CJ in the Media

Oversight in the Evening News

- Internal Affairs
- Investigative Commissions
- Police Commissions
- Citizen Review Boards

Copyright © 2003 Allyn and Bacon

CJ in the World

Oversight of the Police in Britain and France

Copyright © 2003 Allyn and Bacon

CJ in the World

- France has a national police force- easier to regulate police misconduct

- Britain has a national and decentralized police system

Copyright © 2003 Allyn and Bacon

Police

Prosecution of Officers

Police officers in *all jurisdictions* can be prosecuted in criminal court, and police departments and officers can be named in civil suits

Copyright © 2003 Allyn and Bacon

Police Prosecutions

- Police Corruption
- Criminal Prosecution
- Civil Suits against the Police
Negligent training,   Supervision, and Retention   Section 1983 lawsuits   Lawsuits against Federal Agents

Copyright © 2003 Allyn and Bacon

Chapter 6

CRIMINAL JUSTICE
JAMES A. FAGIN

Historical Development of American Policing

Evolution of Policing

Ancient World

2050 B.C.

Code of Hammurabi

oldest surviving set of laws-

Evolution of Policing

Ancient World

2050 B.C.
Code of Hammurabi
- carved in stone, erected in a public place to be read by citizens

Evolution of Policing

Roman Empire

To maintain public order- needed special military units.

Evolution of Policing

Roman Empire

Praetorian guard - to protect the emperor and his property

Urban Cohorts - maintain public order among citizens

Evolution of Policing

Roots of American Policing

England (Middle Ages)

Frankpledge
or tithing system

Evolution of Policing

Tithing | Every male
over age 12 - member
of a tithing

responsible to
defend self and
territory

Evolution of Policing

Tithing

Defended other tithings

The stronger the tithing,
more secure the people

"Safety in Numbers"

Evolution of Policing

Roots of American Policing

Ten tithings = a shire

Person responsible for shire called the "reeve"

Shire-of-the-reef or *sheriff*

Evolution of Policing

Roots of American Policing

Sheriff had the power to summon citizens' assistance - *posse comitatus*

Evolution of Policing

Roots of American Policing

1066 - William the Conqueror demanded the sheriff's allegiance to be to the *crown*, not the people he served

Evolution of Policing

Roots of American Policing

1116 - "Law of Henry"

England - 30 judicial districts

Certain offenses were violation of "King's Peace"

Evolution of Policing

Roots of American Policing

1215 *Magna Carta*

gave protection to English noblemen against illegal seizure of land
(origin of due process)

Evolution of Policing

Crime in the Cities

• Fire-needed night watch to keep watch

• Factories-many people crowded into cities

• Gin-cheap, public drunkenness

Evolution of Policing

Crime in the Cities

- theft catchers- Bow Street Runners

- first paid police force - London Metropolitan Police

Evolution of Policing

Crime in the Cities

Sir Robert Peel Emphasized *preventive crime fighting*

Preventive patrol

Evolution of Policing

American policing

Local law enforcement - "home rule" by states

System of *night watch* adopted

Evolution of Policing

American policing

Selection of officers based on political favors and loyalties

American police officer was armed

Evolution of Policing

American policing

• *South* - slave patrols

•*West* - town marshals, U.S. Marshals, U.S. Army

American Policing

Professional Model

1900s - August Vollmer - reformer and Chief of Police of Berkeley, California

American Policing

August Vollmer

Emphasis on education, professionalism and administrative reform

American Policing

August Vollmer

- Radios in police cars

- College educated officers

- Fingerprints, polygraphs, and performance and intelligence tests

---

American Policing

Federal Law Enforcement

Independent of state and local police systems

Developed after 1900

American Policing

Federal Law Enforcement

- U.S. Marshal Service
- U.S. Postal Investigation Service

American Policing

Federal Law Enforcement

U.S. Secret Service

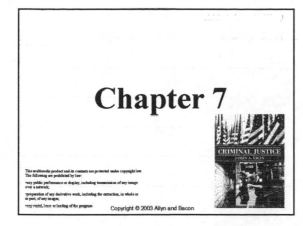

Chapter 7

CRIMINAL JUSTICE
JAMES A. FAGIN

This multimedia product and its contents are protected under copyright law.
The following are prohibited by law:
•any public performance or display, including transmission of any image over a network;
•preparation of any derivative work, including the extraction, in whole or in part, of any images;
•any rental, lease or lending of the program.

Copyright © 2003 Allyn and Bacon

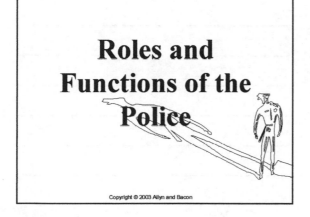

Roles and Functions of the Police

Copyright © 2003 Allyn and Bacon

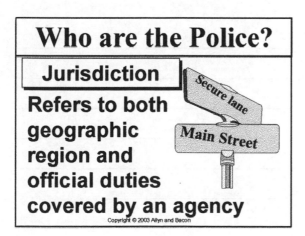

Who are the Police?

Jurisdiction

Refers to both geographic region and official duties covered by an agency

Secure lane
Main Street

Copyright © 2003 Allyn and Bacon

Who are the Police?

County

Law enforcement is performed by the elected office of the Sheriff

SHERIFF

Who are the Police?

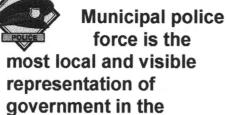

Municipal police force is the most local and visible representation of government in the community

---

Police Patrol

- Variety of services

- Available 24/7

- Serving shifts and Districts

Who are the Police?

Enforce traffic laws and investigate criminal activities

Who are the Police?

Highway Patrol

State police agencies that focus on traffic enforcement

Who are the Police?

Criminal Investigation

Authorized to conduct criminal investigations of state-wide crimes

Who are the Police?

Special Police

Have limited jurisdiction, responsibilities, and powers

Copyright © 2003 Allyn and Bacon

Federal Law Enforcement

Three types of federal law enforcement agencies

Copyright © 2003 Allyn and Bacon

Federal Law Enforcement

- **Military**
- **Civilian**
- **Indian Tribal**

Copyright © 2003 Allyn and Bacon

Federal Law Enforcement

- Agencies are decentralized and fragmented

- Under the administrative control of the Executive Branch of the federal government

Federal Law Enforcement

- Have jurisdiction in all 50 states, District of Columbia and U.S. territories

- Legal jurisdiction often is *overlapping* with both state and local agencies

Criminal Justice in the World

Centralized control and organization of the police

- England- control of 43 provincial police forces

- Chief Constable appointed and a servant of the crown

Criminal Justice in the World

France - Two National Police Agencies

• **National Gendarmerie jurisdiction in towns with population of less than 10,000**

• **French National Police jurisdiction in towns with pop of more than 10,000**

Criminal Justice in the World

France - Two National Police Agencies

• **Recruitment for the two agencies is national, and recruits are State trained**

• **Required to be a French citizen to serve**

• *No local control* **- State run**

Federal Law Enforcement

Military and Tribal Police

•**Military services use military personnel who can make arrests and carry firearms**

•**Military police do preventive patrol, respond to reports of crimes, investigate, and arrest suspects, etc.**

Federal Law Enforcement

Military and Tribal Police

• Each Indian reservation has the authority to establish their own Tribal Police to provide police services

• Police services are also provided by the FBI and the Bureau of Indian Affairs

---

Federal Law Enforcement

Civilian Agencies

• FBI
• U.S. Marshal's Office
• DEA
• ATF
• INS

Who are the Police?

• Duties range from security to high-tech crime fighting

• No one agency responsible for law enforcement in the U.S.

Who are the Police?

Police play a
vital role in
public order,

and it is *constantly changing*

Chapter 8

Police Professionalism and the Community

Impacts of Professionalism on Policing

Selection of Officers

Major influences on police professionalism are the quality of applicants hired and the training they receive

---

Selection of Officers

•No universal hiring process used by local agencies

•No universally required criteria and procedures

Diversity in the System

Civil Rights Act of 1972

Prohibited discrimination in hiring based upon gender, race, and religious affiliation

Diversity in the System

- **Equal Employment Opportunity**

- **Minimum Job Qualifications**

Careers in the System

Qualifications for Police Work

- **Age, Driver's License, Residence**
- **Education**
- **Written Examination**
- **Oral Interview**
- **Medical and Physical Examination**

Qualifications

- **Good Moral Character**

- **Psychological and Polygraph Examination**

Qualifications

Systems are in place to ensure that newly recruited police officers receive the training they need to be effective and professional in their jobs

Training

- Selection for the Academy
- Police Officers Standards and Training Commissions (POST)
- Field Training
- Probationary Period

Policing Strategies

Styles of policing reflect community values and the history of police community relations

Police Styles

- *Watchman:* order maintenance and a great deal of discretion

- *Service:* emphasizes the service role, rather than crime fighting role

- *Legalistic:* strict enforcement of the rules, crime fighter, rule enforcer

Eras of Policing

- **Political Era**

- **Progressive Era**

- **Reform Era**

Criminal Justice and the Media

How accurate is the media's portrayal of the police and police work?

Criminal Justice and the Media

During 1950s-1970s:

Police were identified with the status quo, and the media helped spread this image

Community Policing

Common elements of community policing are proactive police services that emphasized decentralized crime prevention, preventing...

Community Policing

...the reoccurrence of crime, and promoting the quality of life in the community

Community Policing

- **Broken Windows**

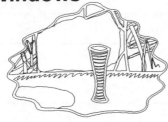

Community Policing

- **Broken Windows**
- **Zero Tolerance**

Ethics in the System

- Police Partnership and Public Order
- Problem-Oriented Policing
- SARA
- Challenges of Community Policing
- Future of Community Policing

Professionalism

- Police Administration and Leadership

- SOP

- Accreditation of Police Departments

- Police Unions and Professional Organization

Copyright © 2003 Allyn and Bacon

Chapter 9

The Court System

The Court System

Hub of the Criminal Justice System

The Court System

All law enforcement and prosecutorial agencies work to move defendants into the court system and…

© Allyn & Bacon 2003

The Court System

…from the courts, defendants are removed from the system if found not guilty, or directed toward correctional agencies

© Allyn & Bacon 2003

The Court System

Dual Court System:

• Federal

• State

© Allyn & Bacon 2003

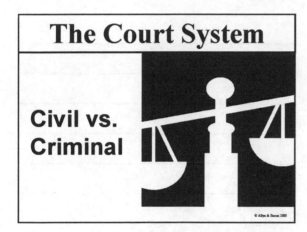

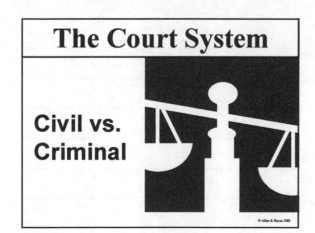

The Court System

Civil Private law - includes redress for harm done to another that is not criminal

Contract law - regulates the varied legal transactions between groups and individuals

© Allyn & Bacon 2003

The Court System

Criminal

Government prosecutes a defendant accused of violating a criminal law

© Allyn & Bacon 2003

The Court System

Federal The federal court system has a hierarchical structure, including lower courts, courts of appeal, and the Supreme Court

© Allyn & Bacon 2003

The Court System

Federal

- United States Supreme Court
- United States Court of Appeals
- United States District Courts
- United States Magistrate's Courts

© Allyn & Bacon 2003

The Court System

State

State courts have jurisdiction to settle legal disputes and criminal matters for violation of local, or state, criminal ordina

© Allyn & Bacon 2003

The Court System

State

- Courts of Last Report
- Appellate Courts
- Courts of General Jurisdiction
- Courts of Limited Jurisdiction

© Allyn & Bacon 2003

Lawyers and Judges

Lawyers must receive legal training and pass the bar exam to practice law

© Allyn & Bacon 2003

Lawyers and Judges

Judges are appointed or elected to positions

© Allyn & Bacon 2003

Ethics in the System

Ethical Violations of Lawyers

- Inquiries into wrongdoing

- Reprimands, corrections of defects

- Disbarment

© Allyn & Bacon 2003

Ethics in the System

Education of Lawyers

- Formal education is 2-3 years of graduate study beyond the bachelors degree

- LSAT requirement

- Pass the state bar examination

Criminal Justice in the World

England

- Criminal cases handled by the Crown Courts

- Heard by a judge and a jury

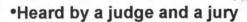

Criminal Justice in the World

England

Two-tier legal profession consisting of solicitors and barristers

Criminal Justice in the World

England Solicitors: provide legal advice to the public and handle other civil matters, such as drawing up contracts, handling probate, and divorces

© Allyn & Bacon 2003

_____

_____

_____

_____

_____

_____

_____

Criminal Justice in the World

England Barristers: Legal specialists who carry on the English tradition of oral arguments to a judge and/or a jury

© Allyn & Bacon 2003

_____

_____

_____

_____

_____

_____

_____

Judicial System

The dual court system of the United States a unified judicial system in which the fundamental rights of all United States citizens are protected

© Allyn & Bacon 2003

_____

_____

_____

_____

_____

_____

Chapter 10

CRIMINAL JUSTICE
JAMES A. FAGIN

This multimedia product and its contents are protected under copyright law. The following are prohibited by law:
-any public performance or display, including transmission of any image over a network;
-preparation of any derivative work, including the extraction, in whole or in part, of any images;
-any rental, lease or lending of the program.

Copyright © 2003 Allyn and Bacon

Courtroom Participants and the Trial

Copyright © 2003 Allyn and Bacon

Adjudication

Criminal trials take place in three types of courts, chosen on the basis of the jurisdiction and severity of the crime

Copyright © 2003 Allyn and Bacon

Trials

Courts of Limited Jurisdiction

Crimes such as
simple assault,
disorderly
conduct,
trespass, and
larceny

Copyright © 2003 Allyn and Bacon

Trials

Courts of Limited Jurisdiction

•No right to an attorney

•Simple trials

•Few witnesses and a
minimum of evidence

Copyright © 2003 Allyn

Trials

**Courts of General Jurisdiction
(state and federal)**

•Which court has jurisdiction?

•Which laws were violated and
the geographic location of the
crime

Trials

Courts of General Jurisdiction (state and federal)

State courts may claim jurisdiction if all or part of the crime is committed within the state

Copyright © 2003 Allyn and Bacon

Trials

Courts of General Jurisdiction (state and federal)

Federal courts claim jurisdiction for crimes committed in the U.S, its territories…

Copyright © 2003 Allyn and Bacon

Trials

Courts of General Jurisdiction (state and federal)

maritime jurisdictional limits, federal, Native American and military reservations, and U.S. registered ships at sea

Copyright © 2003 Allyn and Bacon

Trials

Charges and Proceedings

The police and the prosecutor work together to determine the charges to be brought against the defendant

Copyright © 2003 Allyn and Bacon

Trials

Charges and Proceedings

Also, setting bail, competency to stand trial, and plea bargaining

Copyright © 2003 Allyn and Bacon

Trials

Preparation for Trial

•Defendant has a right to a speedy trial and legal counsel

•Follows specific rules of evidence

Copyright © 2003 Allyn and Bacon

Trials

Preparation for Trial

Proceeds with judge, prosecutor, and jury serving specific roles in the trial

Copyright © 2003 Allyn and Bacon

Trials

Preparation for Trial

- Sixth Amendment right to a speedy trial

- Speedy trial of 1974

Copyright © 2003 Allyn and Bacon

Careers in the System

Court Administrator

- Can be judges or non-lawyer professionals who handle the administrative matters of the court

- No judicial duties, works for the judge, manages the courtroom staff

Copyright © 2003 Allyn and Bacon

Careers in the System

Clerk of the Court

- Works directly with the judge

- Responsible for the court records and issuance of legal documents

- Essential to efficient operation of the court

Copyr. ...03 Allyn and Bacon

Rules of Evidence

Includes procedures called *motions*, which are formal, written requests, requesting...

Copyright © 2003 Allyn and Bacon

Rules of Evidence

...the judge to make a ruling regarding some aspect of the trial prior to the start of the trial

Copyright © 2003 Allyn and Bacon

Pretrial Motions

- Pretrial Motions

- Motion for Continuance
- Motion for Discovery
- Motion for Change of Venue

_____

_____

_____

_____

_____

_____

Pretrial Motions

- Motion for Suppression
- Motion for a Bill of Particulars
- Motions for Severance of Charges or Defendants
- Motion for Dismissal

_____

_____

_____

_____

_____

_____

Participants in the Trial

- Representatives of the government
- Representatives of the defendant
- Witnesses and Victims

_____

_____

_____

_____

_____

_____

Criminal Justice

In the World: France

- Practices Continental law
- Purpose is to *discover the truth*
- Not based on adversarial system as the American trial

Copyright © 2003 Allyn and Bacon

Criminal Justice

In the World: France

Criminal offenses are divided into felonies, misdemeanors and violations

Copyright © 2003 Allyn and Bacon

Criminal Justice

In the World: France

- Investigation of a crime is supervised by the courts, not the police
- Trial of three judges

Copyright © 2003 Allyn and Bacon

Criminal Justice

In the World: France

- Jurors selected by lottery - nine jurors

- Public trial

- Civil damages can be awarded at same trial

Copyright © 2003 Allyn and Bacon

The Trial

Justice is the Goal

Despite the differences among the various courts, all work toward a common objective:

justice

Copyright © 2003 Allyn and Bacon

Chapter 11

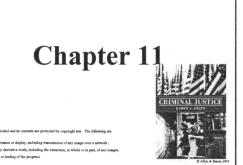

Sentencing and Sanctions

Criminal Sanctions

Criminal sanctions are created to deter, incapacitate, seek retribution, or rehabilitate the offender and restore the community

Criminal Sanctions

- Deterrence
- Incapacitation
- Retribution
- Rehabilitation
- Restorative Justice

Sentencing

- Sentencing by a judge sets the punishment for an offense

- State courts of limited jurisdiction oversee sentencing for misdemeanors

Sentencing

State courts of general jurisdiction and U.S. Magistrates Courts oversee sentencing for felonies

Criminal Justice in the World

Terrorism

When the punishment does not fit the crime

© Allyn & Bacon 2003

Criminal Justice in the World

Terrorism

Terrorist defendants subject to trial by a military tribunal

© Allyn & Bacon 2003

Sentencing

Pre-Sentence Investigation

After a defendant is found guilty, a sentence is determined through a process of presentence investigation and sentencing hearings

© Allyn & Bacon 2003

Sentencing

Pre-Sentence Investigation

A report of information about the defendant to help the judge determine the best sentence

© Allyn & Bacon 2003

Sentencing

Pre-Sentence Investigation

• The completed report (PSI) is forwarded to the judge for review

• Usually contains a recommendation for a particular criminal sanction

© Allyn & Bacon 2003

Sentencing

Sentencing Hearing

Judge sets a date for a sentencing hearing and the prosecution and defense have the opportunity to critique the recommended criminal sanction

© Allyn & Bacon 2003

Sentencing

Victim Impact Statements

- Victims of the crime get an opportunity to influence sentencing

- Very controversial and emotional

Mentally Ill Offenders

Sanctions

The insanity defense exists for defendants who claim that they lack the ability to understand the criminality or harm in their actions

---

Mentally Ill Offenders

Sanctions

Insanity Defense Reform Act-1984

- New standard of insanity

- Defense must demonstrate proof of insanity at the time of the offense by clear and convincing evidence

Mentally Ill Offenders

Insanity Defense

- State Courts have diverse standards of insanity
- Right-Wrong test
- Model penal code
- Guilty but mentally ill

Sentencing Models

Two models that govern the practice of sentencing in courts of general trial jurisdiction are:

- Indeterminate sentencing
- Structured sentencing

Sentencing Models

- *Indeterminate Sentences:* judges give sentences of indeterminate length
- *Determinate Sentences:* defendant is sentenced to a fixed period of time

Sentencing Models

- *Mandatory sentences:* defendants serve their time according to strict application of the law

- *Habitual Offender Laws:* more time for habitual offenders

© Allyn & Bacon 2003

Sentencing Models

The Death Penalty

- Capital punishment is an ongoing issue in American justice
  - Imposition of the death penalty requires special procedures in the courts

© Allyn & Bacon 2003

Sentencing Models

The Death Penalty

Pros and Cons
Issues of:
Civil Rights, Cruel and Unusual Punishment, Innocent Convicted and Executed, Ethics

© Allyn & Bacon 2003

Ethics in the System

The Death Penalty

•Blacks and Hispanics are treated more harshly than whites at every level of the criminal justice system

•Data on the effectiveness of sentencing in reducing crime rates indicate more study is needed

© Allyn & Bacon 2003

_____

_____

_____

_____

_____

_____

_____

Chapter 12

CRIMINAL JUSTICE
JAMES A. FAGIN

Jails and Prisons

Imprisonment: A Modern Invention

Until jails and prisons were built, punishments included branding, mutilation, public ridicule and pain, and whipping

Imprisonment:
A Modern Invention

Societal changes, including industrialization and the growing population of cities…

Copyright © 2003 Allyn and Bacon

Imprisonment:
A Modern Invention

led to the need for prisons as an alternative to enslavement, banishment, and transportation

THE BRITISH CONVICT SHIP SUCCESS OLDEST SHIP AFLOAT, LAUNCHED AT MOULBEIN, BURMAH 1790.

SUCCESS
MELBOURNE

Copyright © 2003 Allyn and Bacon   © Allyn & Bacon 2002

Development of American Jails and Prisons

The American system has developed from a system that abused and exploited prisoners into…

Copyright © 2003 Allyn and Bacon

Development of American Jails and Prisons

...a system that protects prisoner's rights

Institutional racism and Incarceration

Incarceration rates clearly demonstrate that there is a disproportionate confinement rate for minorities

Institutional racism and Incarceration

- White male has a 1 in 23 chance of serving time in prison

- Hispanic male has a 1 in 6 chance

- Black male has a 1 in 4 chance

Jails

Jails are multi-purpose holding facilities and serve as a *gateway* for the criminal justice system

---

Jails: Local

- There are over 3,300 local or county jails

- They vary greatly in size

Jails: Municipal

Most municipalities have abandoned the use of municipal or police jail

State Prisons

State prisons are correctional facilities with different security levels, prisoner classifications and…

State Prisons

…administration models for the incarceration of persons convicted of crimes

Diversity In the System

Women behind Bars

Female offenders have become more common and are routinely housed in separate facilities

Diversity In the System

Women behind Bars

•In 1983, 15,652 women incarcerated serving a year or more

•In 2002, number increased to 85,108

Copyright © 2003 Allyn and Bacon

Security Levels

• Minimum Security Prisons

• Medium Security Prisons

• Maximum and Super-Max Prisons

Copyright © 2003 Allyn and Bacon

Careers In the System

Employment in state prison system – 2 categories

•Professional staff

•Correctional or custodial staff

Copyright © 2003 Allyn and Bacon

Federal Prisons

Federal prisons are correctional facilities for inmates convicted of federal crimes

---

Private Jails and Prisons

Because of overcrowding of correctional facilities and budget problems…

Private Jails and Prisons

…state and federal prisons are being housed in for-profit private jails and prisons

Private Jails and Prisons

Recidivism rates show that jails and prisons have not proven as effective as desired

_____

_____

_____

_____

_____

_____

_____

Private Jails and Prisons

Threats of pain and incarceration have not deterred people from committing crimes, nor rehabilitated most of them

_____

_____

_____

_____

_____

_____

_____

Chapter 13

CRIMINAL JUSTICE
JAMES A. FAGIN

Copyright © 2003 Allyn and Bacon

Probation and Parole

Copyright © 2003 Allyn and Bacon

Why Early Release?

Alternatives to incarceration include diversion for defendants, probation or suspended sentence for convicted offenders…

Copyright © 2003 Allyn and Bacon

Why Early Release?

...and parole
or early
release for
prisoners

Why Early Release?

...and parole
or early
release for
prisoners

Why Early Release?

Mandatory and Good Time Release

•When prisoners serve the entire
length of their sentence, they must
be released - mandatory

•When they have served less than
entire sentence, but have earned
"good time" credit - early release

Why Early Release?

Pardon and Commutation

• Both forms of executive forgiveness

• Pardons - clemency or acts of mercy

• Can be performed by governor for state prisoners and...

Copyright © 2003 Allyn and Bacon

Why Early Release?

Pardon and Commutation

President of the United States for federal and military inmates

Copyright © 2003 Allyn and Bacon

Probation

Has *rehabilitation* as its goal, and allows a convicted defendant to serve time under supervision...

Copyright © 2003 Allyn and Bacon

Probation

….while living in the community, so long as he/she obeys the court-ordered conditions of probation

Copyright © 2003 Allyn and Bacon

Parole

- Provides for the early conditional release of prisoners

- Decided by the parole board

- Supervised in the community by parole officers

Copyright © 2003 Allyn and Bacon

Ethics in the System

Who should know about offenders returning to the community?

Copyright © 2003 Allyn and Bacon

Parole Boards

State Parole Boards

- Each state establishes its own parole board

- Established by legislation and administered by the office of the governor

Parole Boards

Federal Parole Board

- 1976 - United States Parole Commission

- Chairperson and commissioners appointed by the President

- Parole abolished for inmates convicted after 11-1-87

Parole Hearing

- Very brief

- Private, not public

- Held in prison where the prisoner is housed

- Convened by the parole board or a hearing examiner

Parole Conditions

Conditions of parole relate to *security* and to plans for treatment and rehabilitation

Probation and Parole

Careers in the System

- A significant degree of independence in their work

- Work directly with offenders in the office and at their homes

- Potential life threatening situations and considered stressful

Probation and Parole

Careers in the System

- Acts as a case worker to help clients succeed in the reintegration into the community and fulfill the conditions of their release

- Resource broker to help clients obtain services, treatment, and employment

Probation and Parole

Careers in the System

Law enforcement officer and officer of the court empowered to enforce compliance with the court's order and obedience to the law

Probation and Parole

•The criminal justice system invests substantially in keeping offenders out of jails and prisons

•Too many offenders under correctional supervision to house them all in prison

Chapter 14

Prevention and Corrections in the Community

Intermediate Sanctions

Incarceration may get criminals off the street, but its failure to prepare inmates for returning to society....

Intermediate Sanctions

...has resulted in high rates of *recidivism*

Intermediate Sanctions

Community Safety

Communities want offenders to be incarcerated but do not want to provide...

Intermediate Sanctions

Community Safety

...community-based corrections programs for released prisoners in their own neighborhood

Intermediate Sanctions

Community Corrections

Intermediate sanctions were developed as a means of transitioning inmates back to society

Copyright © 2003 Allyn and Bacon

Intermediate Sanctions

Community Corrections

• Intensive Probation Supervision

• Split Sentencing and Shock Probation

• Shock Incarceration: Boot Camps

Copyright © 2003 Allyn and Bacon

Intermediate Sanctions

Community Corrections

Home Confinement and Electronic Monitoring

Copyright © 2003 Allyn and Bacon

Reentry Programs

Taking Responsibility

Prison programs in which inmates participate prior to release can help to ease their transition to life in society as law-abiding citizens

Copyright © 2003 Allyn and Bacon

Reentry Programs

Taking Responsibility

- Work Release
- Education Release
- Halfway Houses
- Day Reporting Centers

Copyright © 2003 Allyn and Bacon

Careers in the System

Correctional Case Manager

- Some on-the-job training
- Training in day-to-day policies and procedures
- Minimum of bachelor's degree-masters preferred

Copyright © 2003 Allyn and Bacon

Reentry for Drug Offenders

The rampant abuse of drugs among offenders has led to a separate system of drug courts and rehabilitation programs

Copyright © 2003 Allyn and Bacon

Reentry for Drug Offenders

- Adult Drug Courts

- Juvenile Drug Courts

- Tribal Drug Courts

Copyright © 2003 Allyn and Bacon

Reentry for Drug Offenders

TASC and RSAT

- Treatment Accountability for Safer Communities

- Residential Substance Abuse Treatment

Copyright © 20..

Reentry for Drug Offenders

TASC and RSAT

- Combines intermediate sanctions and drug offender treatment programs

- To prevent a return to drug use, treatment is provided both in prison and after release

---

Reentry for Drug Offenders

- Combination of treatment strategies can reduce recidivism by about 50%

- Also reduces costs and costs less than incarceration

Try, Try Again

- Many correctional programs, philosophies and challenges are new and evolving

- New intermediate sanctions have focused on control and treatment in the community

Try, Try Again

In the last decade, new programs for addressing the crisis of drug-addicted inmates are winning greater acceptance

Try, Try Again

...by the entire criminal justice system and the public

Try, Try Again

Perfect methods to rehabilitate offenders and to provide for community safety when offenders are released back into the community have not been found

Try, Try Again

The correctional system continues to look for new and better ways to protect the community

Copyright © 2003 Allyn and Bacon

Try, Try Again

...while providing successful reentry of offenders into the community

Copyright © 2003 Allyn and Bacon

Chapter 15

Challenges in the Criminal Justice System

Beyond Crime and Justice

Challenges

•Violent criminality of youthful offenders (school)

•Impacts of illegal drug use and trafficking

Beyond Crime and Justice

Challenges

- Physical and mental health problems in the offender population

- Many new problems and opportunities that spring from developing technology

Copyright © 2003 Allyn and Bacon

Fear of Violent Crimes

No Safe Place

- Violence, particularly *youth violence,* presents a major challenge to the criminal justice system

- Multifaceted causes and sources of violence make the problem hard to solve

Copyright © 2003 Allyn and Bacon

Fear of Violent Crimes

No Safe Place

- Homicides committed by very young offenders

- Brutal juvenile crime

Copyright © 2003 Allyn and Bacon

Violence in the Media

Entertainment or Cause of Crime

"Television viewing can affect the mental, social and physical health of young people"

American Academy of Pediatrics

_____

_____

_____

_____

_____

_____

_____

Violence in Schools

Many students are afraid to attend school, and many parents are concerned for their child's safety at school

_____

_____

_____

_____

_____

_____

_____

Violence in Schools

Accountability

•Public fear of school violence is that its cause is a mystery

•No single profile of a school shooter

_____

_____

_____

_____

_____

_____

Drugs: War on Drugs or Addiction

- Drug-related criminal activity impacts society at many levels

- Different competing strategies exist for dealing with drug use

Copyright © 2003 Allyn and Bacon

Drugs: War on Drugs or Addiction

- Drugs and Crime

- Drug Abuse

- Drugs, Organized Crime and Narcoterrorism

- New Strategies for the War on Drugs

Copyright © 2003 Allyn and Bacon

Offender Physical and Mental Health Challenges

Special concerns about the care of the elderly offender, inmates injured in prison gang violence...

Copyright © 2003 Allyn and Bacon

Offender Physical and Mental Health Challenges

prisoners with HIV/AIDS or TB, offenders with mental illness

Copyright © 2003 Allyn and Bacon

Technology and the Criminal Justice System

Technology has transformed criminal justice, creating new ways to solve problems, creating new types of crime, and raising new constitutional issues

Copyright © 2003 Allyn and Bacon

Technology and the Criminal Justice System

- Computers
- Digital cameras
- Identity theft
- Cybercrime and the Internet
- Cyberporn

Copyright © 2003 Allyn and Bacon

Ethics in the System

Corporate Crime

- White-collar and corporate crime

- Corporate fraud and mismanaging of employee retirement and stock options

Copyright © 2003 Allyn and Bacon

Careers in the System

Computer Security and Cyber Police

- Few full time law enforcement agents to catch cyber criminals

- No police academy training

- Masters degree in computer security needed for employment

Copyright © 2003 Allyn and Bacon

Criminal Justice-21st Century

- Criminal Justice agencies and personnel will be needed to perform new roles and responsibilities

- Police will need new skills and corrections will need new tools to deal with offenders and monitor them in the community

Copyright © 2003 Allyn and Bacon

Criminal Justice-21st Century

- Legislatures will define new crimes and pass new police powers

- Concerns such as Internet use, terrorism, DNA evidence, and privacy rights will emerge

Criminal Justice-21st Century

Mandatory national identification cards, anti-terrorist security measures and drug laws will be developed

Criminal Justice-21st Century

Threat of terrorism will result in an expansion of police powers, challenges to Constitutional rights, and the creation of new criminal justice and antiterrorism agencies

NOTES

NOTES

NOTES